Our Favorite Verses

Tina Ware-Walters, PhD
(Compiler and Editor)

Our Favorite Verses

TINA WARE-WALTERS, PhD
(Compiler and Editor)

OUR FAVORITE VERSES
Copyright © 2015 by Tina Ware-Walters, PhD

Published by:

Healthy Life Press • 9375 Blue Mountain Drive • Golden, CO 80403
www.healthylifepress.com

Compiler and Editor: Tina Ware-Walters, PhD
Designer: Judy Johnson

Printed in the United States of America

No part of this publication may be reproduced, stored in a retrieval system, or transmitted in any form or by any means—for example, electronic, photocopy, recording—without the prior written permission of the author, except for brief quotations in printed reviews.

Library of Congress Cataloging-in-Publication Data
Ware-Walters, Tina
Our Favorite Verses

ISBN 978-1-939267-91-7
1. Bibles (Multiple Translations) – Devotional; 2. Christian Life – Inspirational

Undesignated Scripture references are taken from THE HOLY BIBLE, NEW INTERNATIONAL VERSION®, NIV®, Copyright© 1973, 1978, 1984, 2011 by Biblica, Inc.™ Scriptures marked NKJV are from the New King James Version, copyright© 1982 by Thomas Nelson, Inc. Used by permission. All rights reserved worldwide. Scriptures marked NASB are from the New American Standard Bible, copyright © 1960, 1962, 1963, 1968, 1971, 1972, 1973, 1975, 1977, 1995 by The Lockman Foundation. Used by permission. Scriptures marked NRSV are from the New Revised Standard Version, copyright © 1989 by the Division of Christian Education of the National Council of the Churches of Christ in the United States of America. Used by permission. All rights reserved. Scriptures marked NAB are from the New American Bible, revised edition © 2010, 1991, 1986, 1970 by the Confraternity of Christian Doctrine, Inc., Washington, DC. All Rights Reserved. Scriptures marked KJV are from the King James Version of the Bible, which is in the public domain.

Capitalization of pronouns related to deity follows *The Christian Writer's Manual of Style* (Grand Rapids: Zondervan, 2004). In biblical quotes, capitalization of pronouns related to deity follows the translation in use.

The opinions expressed in this book are those of the contributors and may not represent the official position of Healthy Life Press, its publisher, or any of its other authors.

Contents

Preface

COMFORT

Living By The Word Rebecca Luttrell Briley, PhD	3
God's Immeasurable Power Tina Ware-Walters, PhD	11
Praising God Through Pain Robin Lashley	15
God's Friendship Emily Lindsey	19
The Strong Support of Friends Gwenn Quinn	23
In The Hands of God Kay Crouch	27
Rejoicing Versus Sorrow Debby McCrary	35
Finding Strength in Scriptures Loretta Parrish	39
God's Grace Jennifer Escobar	43
For My Fellow Worriers Tina Ware-Walters, PhD	47
The Healing Power of God's Word Jolene Schmidt	51
Our Little Fisherman Jacci Gantz	55

PERSPECTIVE

Attitude Adjustment James D. Dvorak, PhD	61

BUDDY, CAN YOU SPARE A DOLLAR? Tim Dallas	67
HOW HAS GOD BEEN GOOD TO YOU THIS WEEK? Sarah Hinds	69
HOPE FROM FORGIVENESS Gina Simpson	73
RELAXING IN GRACE Charles Rix, PhD	75
IS THAT OUR CHURCH? Gina Simpson	81
SEARCH INSIDE FIRST Berlin Fang	83
INSPIRED BY THE GOOD SAMARITAN Deacon Jerry Rakosky	87
GOOD EXAMPLES Matthew Walters	91

QUICK INSPIRATION

VERSES TO CARRY YOU THROUGH CHALLENGES Holli Potts-Boedeker	99
WONDERFULLY MADE Melanie Hawley	101
WHAT REALLY MATTERS Debby McCrary	103
GOD'S AMAZING LOVE Myra McCrary Moran	105
SOME OF MY FAVORITE VERSES FOR SIN AND WORRY Ed Estes	107
TRUST I. Reily	109
BEAUTY Paige Bailey	111
FEAR NOT Laura McCrary	113
NOTES	114
ABOUT THE AUTHORS	115
HEALTHY LIFE PRESS RESOURCES	122

Preface

ONE DAY, AFTER HAVING BEEN SICK FOR SEVERAL MONTHS, I FELT ESPECIALLY frustrated and down. I prayed for help and was reminded how Ephesians 3:20 had been particularly encouraging to me during a stressful time in my life a few years before. I thought that if I had a favorite verse and a personal story to match how that particular Scripture had helped me, then others probably did, too. And, if I wanted to read those stories, others might want to as well. I asked friends, family, colleagues, and even bloggers I had never met to contribute their stories about how a particular verse or set of verses had helped them, and *Our Favorite Verses* was born.

Throughout my two-year illness, reading the stories that people sent raised my spirits and I know they helped in my recovery. Each day that I opened my e-mail and found a new story from someone I healed a bit more. And I looked forward to the day when more people could read this collection of inspiring, comforting accounts sent in by Christians from all over the country.

The contributors to *Our Favorite Verses* vary in age, gender, background, education, and occupation, including: PhD's, stay-at-home moms, prominent bloggers, published authors, grandmothers, and grandfathers. But they all have something in common, which is that each of them has a beautiful story of how a particular Scripture has impacted their lives.

Our Favorite Verses is divided into three sections: "Comfort," "Perspective," and "Quick Inspiration." Stories of triumph over adversity such as job loss, depression, and infertility will inspire you in the "Comfort" section. As you read these stories you will be reminded that anything is possible with God in control. "Perspective" focuses on living a better Christian life. The authors' personal accounts show the effect of adopting a "God's eye" view in this fallen world. "Quick Inspiration" is comprised of short messages for those on-the-go, harried days when you only have a couple of minutes for devotionals. Each thought is a quick shot of encouragement to jumpstart your day.

So, whether you need comfort, discernment, or a quick devotional, *Our Favorite Verses* will help you on your journey of faith. As you connect with each story, you will enjoy a deeper understanding of how God continues to work in lives through the Bible today, and this could become a great source of encouragement as you make your way through the pages that follow.

Some of the stories will make you teary-eyed, in a good way, or remind you that with God anything is possible. Others will motivate you to live a better Christian life. All of them will make you think. As a result, you may pause and recall what your own favorite verse is and how God has made its truth personal for you.

In any case, as you read, I hope you gain as much from the accounts in *Our Favorite Verses* as I have. And if you do, please feel free to share your own favorite verse with me, so that can perhaps become part of the next collection!

~ Tina Ware-Walters, PhD
(Compiler and Editor)

COMFORT

Who doesn't love a good victory story? You know the kind; it begins with the character encountering seemingly impossible challenges and ends with an emotional triumph. The first section of "Comfort" consists of twelve inspirational stories about women who have faced challenging life storms such as divorce, cancer, and infertility. Each account tells the ways that God comforted the author through Scripture, carried them through their difficulties, and made them stronger.

Several authors point to verses from Psalms. One story describes a mother and wife who battled a brain tumor with the overwhelming support of her family and friends as she learned the true meaning of Psalm 27:1: "The Lord is my light and salvation, whom shall I fear?"

Another tells of a stay-at-home mother whose husband loses his job and the family's health insurance the night before their infant daughter's costly surgery. The mother prayed and pleaded Psalm 6:8 to God: "Away from you, all who do evil, for the Lord has heard my weeping . . ." and God answered her in a remarkable way.

Other accounts point to Hebrews, Philippians, and 1 Peter as well as other books of the Bible. While some of the stories deal with similar topics or verses, each stands out as an extraordinary testament to God's ability to comfort through rough times and to turn pain and sadness into joy and glory to him.

Living by the Word

by Rebecca Luttrell Briley, PhD

SCRIPTURE HAS BEEN AN INTEGRAL PART OF MY LIFE FOR AS LONG AS I can remember. I memorized Bible verses before I could read: My mother would repeat them over and over to me until I knew them; then I would recite them in front of my little country church to everyone's approval. I will never forget the first verse I learned: *"The heavens declare the glory of God; and the firmament sheweth his handiwork"* (Psalm 19:1, KJV). "Firmament" was a hard word to pronounce, and "sheweth" in the King James, which was the only translation we had at the time, looked and sounded funny. Still, the importance of Scripture was deeply implanted in me at an early age, and I grew up loving and marveling at God's creation in the beautiful scenery of rural Kentucky where I spent my childhood. Many more verses followed, most of which I still remember, but Psalm 19 will always hold that special "first" spot in my memory.

One other verse does stand out, though, as I continued to grow "in wisdom and stature" (see Luke 2:52). My parents were strict in their discipline and stringent in their expectations of my sister and me, spiritually as well as in all other aspects of our young lives. Although we grew up with few material possessions, my mother insisted we had much to be thankful for, calling attention to the fact that our "little" seemed a great deal when compared to that of so many of our neighbors. She always filled boxes with our used toys and hand-me-down clothing—often before we were even finished with them—and added canned goods and other staples to be delivered to the more impoverished in our community. Much to our chagrin, my sister and I had to carry the boxes to the selected doors and knock, while my mother waited unseen in our car by the side of the road. It was her idea to donate the boxes; why did we have to be the ones to deliver them? We complained, resenting the embarrassing position in which it often placed us. "It is to teach you charity," Mom explained, though I realize now she probably did not want to humiliate the recipients further by having to face her in their need, our indignity disregarded. She understood that Kentuckians are proud people, reluctant to accept assistance, even in times of desperate hardship.

"You have been given much, and to whom much has been given, much shall be required," was how she paraphrased Luke 12:48. Whether it appeared to be "much" to me or not, God had entrusted me with so much more than the average person; he expected me to live up to his requirement. This verse came to epitomize the great expectations I learned to have of myself, instilled by my parents' high standards in all things, not just spiritual. In school, an A- wasn't good enough; club membership wasn't acceptable if there was an office to be filled. Anything but first place equaled just an "also ran"—in other words, a failure. Spurred by my parents' ambition for their children, I came to expect only the absolute best of myself, assuming God would accept no less. I may have heard the term "unconditional love," but I certainly did not apply it to my situation. God, my parents—even I—could not love me if I did not give everything I had all the time.

This relentless ambition took its toll. When I made a mistake, mortification overtook me. If I came in second, I cried in shame. I had such anxiety in contests and competitions (which I was compelled to enter), I developed a nervous habit of pulling my hair or biting my cuticles until they bled. Moreover, if I disappointed God by not living up to his directive in Luke 12:48, I worried I would go to hell or at least miss hearing him say on Judgment Day, "Well done, good and faithful servant!" (Matthew 25:21). I took literally the instruction to donate one coat (or doll or crayon) if I had two, and I gave away my lunch money if anyone asked (and they did, discovering my soft heart). I went without, even when I didn't have to—hoping to please, praying to measure up in all things.

Such a driven young person might be difficult to live with; however, my extreme paradigm was for myself alone. Somehow at an early age, I adopted Luke 12:48 as my particular mantra, not meant for anyone else, including my sister. I shrugged off others' lack of ambition, failures, or selfishness, supposing God didn't command so much of them—only of me. In retrospect, I realize now such an elite attitude negated Micah 6:8, which spells out God's actual "requirement" of all of humanity: "He hath showed thee, O man, what is good; and what doth the LORD require of thee, but to do justly, and to love mercy, and to walk humbly with thy God?" (KJV). Humility may not figure into one's assessment of herself when she assumes she has been given much, although I was humbled often, as keeping up with my own high standards was a daunting—and unreachable—task. Too often, worn out by my impossible perfectionism, I identified with Paul's "O wretched man that I am!" (Romans 7:24, KJV), rather than with all those others who were simply happy in the Lord.

Any such pressurized lifestyle is a bomb waiting to explode. My date with destiny, so to speak, arrived when my thirty-five-year-old husband died of brain cancer. I had been so surprised but grateful to God for bringing Kyle and me together, demonstrating his love for me through the exceptional love of such a worthy man as Kyle. My mother still compares him with David, "a man after [God's] own heart" (Acts 13:22). I almost believed such love was my initial evidence of the aforementioned "unconditional," as I knew I couldn't possibly deserve such a perfect gift, and I felt incessantly grateful. So when he received the diagnosis of inoperable malignant brain tumor on our tenth wedding anniversary, I blamed myself. I knew such tragedy had to be the consequence of something I had done, or not done, that displeased God. Even when I begged God for healing, I sensed I had no right to ask; my mother even admonished me that I had to be willing to give Kyle up, as only then would I be worthy of God's favor. So much given, so much required.

"Some gave all," the slogan says, referring to those who have died in service to our country. Giving up Kyle was a greater sacrifice than losing my own life—indeed, I would have preferred to be the one to die instead and often prayed for that exchange. But another adage says, "The good die young," and I knew I wasn't good enough. Much was required, but apparently had not yet been contributed. Kyle, however, was the best I had to give. He was Abel's harvest; he was Abraham's Isaac, without the provided substitute. Yes, "the Lord gave, and the Lord hath taken away" (Job 1:21, KJV), but that was as far as I was going to go. Quite bluntly, I'd had it. Sure, God could do whatever he wanted to do, with or without reason, but in doing so, he certainly didn't prove he loved me. In fact, having to give Kyle back only solidified my belief that God's love was just as conditional as that of my parents.

> When my husband received the diagnosis of inoperable malignant brain tumor on our tenth wedding anniversary, I blamed myself.

When sympathizers tried to comfort me with, "God wanted Kyle with him," I didn't argue. I could certainly understand God's wanting the companionship of such a man after his own heart; he obviously, though, didn't want *me*. If he loved *me*, as he claimed, he would have taken me, too—or at least left Kyle with me. All I was good for was to give and give and give. It was never enough. But I couldn't give any more. I was spent, depleted. I had given all I had and it still didn't satisfy.

The next decade was not an easy or a happy one. Reckless and resentful, I vacillated between anger and despair. What difference did anything make? I had always been such a good girl, but I had still been stripped of everything. So what? God was obviously going to do whatever he wanted anyway, but so was I. It was my turn now, and I didn't care if he liked it or not. Moreover, I didn't care if I survived or not; in fact, I hoped I didn't. I didn't have anything to live for any more, and I just didn't care. Car accidents, broken bones, bouts with malaria, destructive relationships—people began to question if I had a death wish.

Consciously or not, of course I did. Who wouldn't?

Even though I was still in my thirties, my life was over—it just stuttered on like a misfiring engine dieseling after the ignition has been turned off. I had no hope, no future, no light shining at the end of the long, dark interminable tunnel my feet now stumbled through. The only thing that kept me breathing was knowing I could end it all any time I liked, if I was willing to swallow the pills or pull the trigger. And I was willing, though the flesh was naturally weak.

Friends and colleagues used to compliment me on my courage, admiring how I soldiered on in the face of such calamity. Their platitudes infuriated me. What other choice did I have? It wasn't courage; it was endurance. For, like Hamlet, conscience made me a coward, too. They purported envy at my trips around the world, my "exciting adventures in exotic places," failing to notice I simply swung from one dying star to the next, arriving at just another black hole every time. I seethed at their oblivion, suspecting it excused their lack of support. Couldn't they see I was not waving, but drowning?

I had been traveling around the world, literally, for over a decade, teaching here, directing plays there, unwilling to put down roots anywhere, when the opportunity to apply for a permanent faculty position at Oklahoma Christian University was listed in the daily update I got in my inbox from *The Chronicle of Higher Education*. Living in Hawaii at the time, I certainly had no desire to ever settle down in the land-locked American Midwest, but I somehow felt obliged to send in my application: I had been brought up in the Church of Christ, I actually knew someone who lived in Edmond, and I had claimed years ago I wanted to teach creative writing at a private university. Even when I accepted OC's invitation for a campus visit and personal interviews, I had no intention of taking the position should it be offered. I was just going through the motions, confident I wasn't what they were looking for any more than they were my Holy Grail. In fact, I was planning on relocating to Singapore in a couple of months to teach for their Ministry of Education, or returning to Lithuania to the Christian university for which I had been teaching *pro bono* for the past several summers. Singapore, Lithuania, or Oklahoma? For me, America had become anticlimactic.

But God had other ideas. And he enlightened me of those through the next Scripture verse he brought to my awareness. *"'For I know the plans I have for you," declares the Lord, "plans to prosper you . . . to give you hope and a future"'* (Jeremiah 29:11). I first noticed the quote while thumbing through a mail-order catalogue advertising plaques, jewelry, and other gift items. It caught my attention because it was the only "religious" item in the otherwise secular pamphlet. After that, I noticed the same quote on a car's bumper sticker while waiting at a stoplight. Next, it arrived in the mail on a note card from a new friend, and then, just a few days later, on a bookmark from my sister. At a local craft fair, I was astonished to see it as a caption underneath a beautiful photograph of a Hawaiian rainbow! I had never noted this passage before, and now it seemed I was being bombarded by it.

Two words in particular stood out: *prosper* and *future*. If I were to take the Singapore job, I knew I would prosper financially, but I was very uncertain of how long I would want to stay, as I had never visited there and had no idea if I would like the culture and climate. As for the Lithuania position, I knew I loved the location and the people, but I was also aware there could be no long-term future investment. The university operated as a mission where American professors could donate their time and talents while on sabbaticals or during other vacation periods; the best the institute had to offer was a free room in the dorm for the duration of my commitment. Oklahoma, on the other hand, represented both. Though I probably would not become wealthy teaching at OC, I would be able to live comfortably and also regain my tenure, a security I had carelessly thrown away to travel the world after my husband died. With both *prosper* and *future*, there could be *hope*, as well—hope I thought had been buried with Kyle.

Many people, including those at OC, were incredulous when they learned I was choosing to move from Hawaii to Oklahoma. When I told them it was because of the job, several still scratched their heads in bewilderment. What I didn't tell them was that I had gotten a message from God. No, I didn't hear voices in the middle of the night; I wasn't struck down blind on the road to somewhere else. God spoke to me through his Word, perhaps the most reliable way for us to hear and understand him. With my earlier verse, I may have been too young to comprehend it properly, taking it too literally or too personally to apply it effectively to my life.

Older, wiser—sadder, even—I bring some perspective to this new verse that should help me be more discerning. Prosperity and a future may still be years away, but this time there is hope. And, as it says in Romans 5:5: "hope does not disappoint."

God's Immeasurable Power[1]

by Tina Ware-Walters, PhD

A FEW YEARS AGO WHEN I WAS GOING THROUGH A ROUGH PERIOD, I stumbled upon Ephesians 3:20, which says "Now to him who is able to do immeasurably more than all we ask or imagine, according to his power that is at work within us." This became my signature verse. The verse reminded me of God's incredible, amazing power. The words gave me strength and helped me through my most trying year.

The first time I read Ephesians 3:20 closely and committed it to memory, I was thirty-two years old and separated. The survival of my marriage seemed doubtful and I was scared. I desperately needed God's help. My signature verse gave me hope. When I began praying daily for God to work out my situation better than I could ask or imagine, I thought God would give me what I wanted: a rebuilt marriage. Unfortunately, the marriage could not be saved. Nevertheless, I kept praying Ephesians 3:20 and for God's will about everything, my marriage, in particular, and also smaller concerns. God amazed me with his wonderful solutions. However, my life got harder before it got easier.

During the divorce proceedings, my attorney informed me I

would be leaving the marriage economically worse than when I had entered it. I was getting divorced and my financial situation was in trouble. At times I would wonder how God was going to work such a mess into something good. Could he make my life something better than I envisioned? The situation looked impossible to me. I kept praying Ephesians 3:20 and asking God to work out the divorce and my financial situation "better than all I could ask or imagine." Throughout even the worst times, he gave me glimmers of hope with what seemed like miracles, like a friend a calling or stopping by at just the right time, or getting an unexpected work bonus. Those mini miracles carried my faith through to the end.

After several months my divorce dragged on and I was still worried about money, but God provided. He filled my life with supportive friends and family who continually showed his love, and parents who offered to help out financially if necessary. My friends and family made me feel loved and wanted more than ever. Soon, my nightmare was over.

About the time the new year began, my divorce finalized and my financial circumstances improved. A year later God brought a wonderful man into my life and now I have the loving, stable Christian marriage I had always wanted. A year after we married, I counted the money we had received from bonuses, my getting to teach summer school, and other surprise money we received during that twelve months. It totaled exactly what I had lost before. In a short time God had given me my dream husband, he had repaid the money I thought was gone forever, and my spouse

> When I began praying daily for God to work out my situation better than I could ask or imagine, I thought God would give me what I wanted.

and I were more financially secure than either of us had been in our adult lives. Ephesians 3:20 taught me to ask God not just for help but to work situations out better than I can imagine because I dream too small. God is God, after all, the God of miracles!

Nine years have passed and I still pray Ephesians 3:20, that God will do "immeasurably more than I can ask or imagine" every time I am worried or encounter a condition that seems impossible. Every time God has provided me with an awesome solution. Sometimes the solution is the one I think I want, sometimes it isn't. However, the answer is always the best one because it's God's.

Praising God Through Pain

by Robin Lashley

> *Rejoice in the Lord always. I will say it again: Rejoice! Let your gentleness be evident to all. The Lord is near. Do not be anxious about anything, but in everything, by prayer and petition, with thanksgiving, present your requests to God. And the peace of God, which transcends all understanding, will guard your hearts and your minds in Christ Jesus. Finally, brothers, whatever is true, whatever is noble, whatever is right, whatever is pure, whatever is lovely, whatever is admirable—if anything is excellent or praiseworthy—think about such things. Whatever you have learned or received or heard from me, or seen in me—put it into practice. And the God of peace will be with you* (Philippians 4:4-9).

T HIS IS ONE OF MY FAVORITE SECTIONS OF SCRIPTURE, AND IT CAN be applied to any situation, no matter how big or how small. If we as Christians remembered these verses every day, our influence on this world would be so far-reaching. I truly believe we see Christ the most when we are at peace in the midst of a terrible storm.

When I was twenty-four years old, I went through a challenging "storm" that came out of nowhere. My husband of four years was in his first year of law school and living for the first time outside of the "Christian bubble;" it was his first time outside of the private Christian school and private Christian college he'd attended. Many other factors, which I won't mention, contributed to this "storm." Basically, he told me he had never really loved me when we were dating, and felt pressured into getting married, and that now he wanted out. He said he also he wasn't sure about God and the Bible, etc. He felt like he had been placed into a mold his entire life that didn't fit him. After almost an entire year of roller coaster back and forth decisions, moving in and out, and counseling, we finalized our divorce.

I would love to say I clung to the verses in Philippians EVERY day, and knew God had a plan for me this entire time, that I just needed to trust him, and be faithful and rejoice in the blessings of each day. But when I think back on the whirlwind year of 2007, I just don't remember.

But, I did find immense comfort in God's Word, and in Philippians 4. I remember WANTING to really feel the "peace of God which transcends all understanding, that would guard my heart and mind." I was brutally honest with God, and let him know I didn't feel that way, but that I wanted to, badly!

Verses 8 and 9 helped me get through the fire without still smelling like smoke. God taught me through these verses to focus on the good things and blessings all around me, and on how I could be serving others who are also hurting . . . rather than dwelling on me, me, me. He showed me that by putting into practice the way Jesus lived (to the best of my human ability) my heart would heal, and I needed to fill my heart with love for others, instead of sorrow for myself.

Now, I did not ignore my own hurt and push my emotions aside... God did plenty of molding, breaking and pounding on my clay jar! I just stopped spending 100 percent of my time lamenting!

I learned the healthy way to "fake it till you make it"—in rejoicing always, and thinking of the good things through laughter and thankfulness. Smiling when I didn't feel like it, and forcing a laugh—even when there was nothing to laugh about—were healing. Almost no one can smile or laugh and still be sad.

> He showed me that by putting into practice the way Jesus lived (to the best of my human ability) my heart would heal, and I needed to fill my heart with love for others, instead of sorrow for myself.

The more I focused on rejoicing, the more happiness I experienced. I realized God does not promise happiness to anyone. Happiness is a choice. Happiness comes in obeying God's word, and if we always are looking for the good in any situation, we will have peace. And, the more we know God, as opposed to knowing of him, the more we trust him, and we realize we have nothing to worry or be anxious about. Simply, put, if we worry, we show a lack of trust in him.

The Spirit is helping me each day to rejoice, no matter how bad the circumstance, and the journey is amazing. I am thankful for the storm and for the rain that brought so much growth and nourishment to my soul. Praise God!

God's Friendship

by Emily Lindsey

Throughout my life, my friendships have taken me on an emotional roller coaster; I have experienced the highs and the lows, consequences of my actions, as well as those of my friends. I've always longed for a couple of really good girlfriends with whom I could be open and honest, with whom I could form such lasting relationships that no matter where life took us, we'd always stay close. I knew I needed spiritual encouragement from other girls my age from the way I felt such a thirst for these imaginary girlfriends. I am the youngest of six girls, with significant age differences among all of us, the gap between me and the closest in age being five years. Because of this large age gap, I didn't experience the kind of friendship with my sisters I wanted—we were separated by different stages in life. I lacked girlfriends my age at church, as well; growing up surrounded by peers predominantly male made me feel lonely and isolated, especially since my friends at public school didn't share my faith.

With this background, it is understandable to see why I was so encouraged upon entering a Christian university I attended and finding so many girlfriends who were strong Christians. They had had a completely different high school experience! I was elated.

> God allows this sense of loneliness to persist in my heart at times because he knows I need it to gently turn me back to him.

However, although these girls were wonderful, I found I could only get so close with them before reaching a wall. These girls had all grown up together, and had already formed the very bonds I had been yearning for throughout elementary, middle, and high school. I couldn't get in. My sense of discouragement grew as they invested less and less effort into our friendship. I sensed a sort of contrived excitement to greet me each time we saw each other. I was heartbroken. Yet through my tears and disappointment, God allowed me to discern those whose friendships were genuine and remind me, yet again, that his friendship is the only one I need.

I believe with all my heart God allows this sense of loneliness to persist in my heart at times because he knows I need it to gently turn me back to him. I tend to lose focus of what friendships really matter and he allows me to experience loneliness at times because it causes me to seek to him. Friends will inevitably let me down from time to time, even the most genuine and the most loyal, but God is not capable of disappointing. It is not in his nature. When I was feeling especially lonely and discouraged, I found this Psalm, which comforted my hurt feelings and wiped away my tears.

The righteous cry out, and the Lord hears them; he delivers them from all their troubles. **The Lord is close to the brokenhearted and saves those who are crushed in spirit.** *A righteous man may have many troubles, but the Lord delivers him from them all; he protects all his bones, not one of them will be broken* (Psalm 34:17-20, emphasis added).

Yes, others I considered good friends have hurt me and let me down, but my God is always with me and he understands my troubles. He is my comforter and my ideal friend. We are human and we will all at some point let each other down. Therefore, we must remember to put our trust in God and not in men. *In you I trust, o my God* (Psalm 25:1). He is the only one in whom we can fully and securely place our trust. So often I lose sight of this and find (often through pain and disappointment) that I lost sight of what truly matters. I have not always done what Psalm 105:4 says, *look to the Lord and his strength; seek his face always.* Seek his face always. The moment we stop doing that is the moment we become hurt, discouraged, weakened. Yet when we find ourselves in a dark place, the Lord is right with us; *the Lord is close to the brokenhearted and saves those who are crushed in spirit.*

The Strong Support of Friends[2]

by Gwenn Quinn

> *So it came about when Moses held his hand up, that Israel prevailed, and when he let his hand down, Amalek prevailed. But Moses' hands were heavy. Then they took a stone and put it under him, and he sat on it; and Aaron and Hur supported his hands, one on one side and one on the other. Thus his hands were steady until the sun set. So Joshua overwhelmed Amalek and his people with the edge of the sword* (Exodus 17:11-13, NASB).

NOT LONG AFTER THE ISRAELITES HAD COME INTO THE WILDERNESS after fleeing Egypt, a man named Amalek, a descendant of Esau (Jacob's brother), came against the Israelites with his army. The Israelites didn't have a lot of weapons of warfare with them . . . they had left Egypt with only what they could carry. What they had, however, was the staff of God, which Moses carried.

So Moses told Joshua that he would position himself on the hill and hold up the staff during the battle, even as he had held it up to part the Red Sea while the Israelites walked through.

As Joshua and his army came against Amalek and his army, they were victorious as long as Moses held the staff up. But like most battles, it was long and arduous, and Moses' arm got tired. A few times, he laid it down to rest his weary arm, and immediately, Amalek got the upper hand. So Moses' brother Aaron and another man named Hur stationed themselves on either side of Moses, and held his arms up so that Joshua was victorious.

> Many times I've looked at her and wondered if my parenting has had any impact at all. I have felt, more often than not, that I have failed as a mother.

This story has become very personal to me recently. As a mom, I'm wrapping up seventeen years with my oldest daughter, who goes away to college on the other side of the country in about three weeks. And these last two years have been among the most difficult I've ever had with my daughter ... not because she's not a good kid ... but because she's tried me in ways I've never had to deal with before. As she's readied herself for adulthood, she's kicked hard against the womb of my protection, my counsel and my discipline. She wants to get *out*, to be delivered into her new life, into her new freedom, but at the same time, she wants me to run around and help keep all her plates in the air so they don't come crashing down. She wants to be treated like an equal, and doesn't want to keep following the rules, or to do what I ask. We have had a number of very painful fights—loud, angry, ugly fights.

Many times I've looked at her and wondered if my parenting has had any impact at all. I have felt, more often than not, that I have failed as a mother. It is during these times that I have turned to my "Aaron" and my "Hur" so that they can hold my arms up, because I feel like I am so tired and I can't hold them up by myself anymore. And these friends have been there for me, counseling me, encouraging me, and giving me a fresh perspective.

Last night, one of these dear friends was standing with me in my driveway chatting, and my daughter came out briefly from the house to retrieve something from her car. I asked her a question and she answered it thoughtfully. When she went back in the house, my friend looked at me and said, "She's a good kid. She's going to be fine. There are some things you can just tell by observing people."

Those few words meant a lot. It was a pat on the back to me, a support of my arms. It renewed my strength to push on, and finish well.

Everywhere around you are people . . . mothers, fathers, and even single people who have a battle in their lives, and like Moses, they're holding out the staff of God—their faith and their convictions—to win the battle. But it's easy to get weary. If you know what's going on in their lives, do what you can to support them. Even simply checking in with them to let them know you're praying for them makes a huge difference. My same friend sent me a text the other day to ask me how it was going, and to let me know her prayers were ongoing. It was huge. I felt renewed, just knowing someone was helping to bear my burdens.

In the Hands of God

by Kay Crouch

I RARELY HAVE HEADACHES, BUT I STARTED TO EXPERIENCE SOME every few days. The Tylenol bottle and I became friends as I plunged through the hectic Christmas season of 1989. My prayers centered on my mother, who had recently fallen and was in and out of hospitals, but privately, I complained about having this "inconvenience" of headaches in my life. I did not know of my brain tumor or how it would teach me the true meaning of Psalm 27.

The holiday season ended, my mother left the hospital and she and Dad returned home, and I went to my yearly check-up exam with my OB/GYN. I easily passed his test, but I told him that Tylenol and I had become TOO friendly. He asked me if my family was having difficulty. After I explained my busy December schedule, he said I probably had stress headaches. Great! I had never had stress headaches, but whatever. He casually said that if they continued I should consult a neurologist.

I'm going to be real honest with you here. God has richly blessed my life with radiant health. Who was he kidding? I couldn't even SPELL neurologist and I certainly didn't want to talk to one! Surely the stress would disappear soon.

Unfortunately, the headaches continued to the point of causing a few bouts of nausea. In February, I opted to see a headache specialist for about six weeks. Since my "stress" was no longer a problem, I thought the headaches must be migraines, but I went to a neurologist anyway.

After the physical exam, the neurologist said he certainly did not think I had cancer, so he started me on heavy migraine medications. The headaches became daily occurrences. Over the next three to four months, I began to eliminate activities until my schedule reduced to church, Bible study, my rocking chair, and carpool. By May and June, I began using the wrong words in sentences. My family knew I was on a stronger dosage of migraine medicine and would laugh and dismiss it. Sometimes I noticed the word difficulty and sometimes I didn't. These things did not occur often, but my neurologist said these things could certainly be a reaction to the medicine.

I didn't want to have an MRI (magnetic resonance imaging) because I knew it would cost mega-bucks and I didn't want to spend my husband's money to look at a migraine headache. However, when my cousin from Longview called and I kept saying, "I'll mail your son's 'wedding' gift (instead of 'graduation' gift)." She immediately called my best friend, Gwynel, and said, "Get her help!" I was not aware of the word exchange or my cousin's panic. My husband, Bob, and Gwynel went with me to my doctor's appointment and they insisted on a date for an MRI exam. It was set for June 18, 1990.

Since I had scheduled my MRI and with my doctor's permission, I drove to East Texas for a few days to visit my parents. I slept late and watched game shows on TV without dressing. My Dad knew something was wrong, but he didn't know what. He insisted my favorite uncle drive me back me back home when I felt ready to return. I protested, but Daddy wouldn't budge. He said he would follow in his car and bring my uncle back home. I enjoyed being driven back even though I didn't think I needed it. Originally, I had planned to stay a week but I stayed eleven days. I had to return to be available for my lovely MRI exam.

The exam took from 2:30 to 3:30 pm. About 7:15 that evening my neurologist called and asked us to come to the hospital by 8 pm to discuss the imaging results. I still was not concerned. I just figured he worked late like many other doctors.

My neurologist had NO pleasant words for us. The pictures stunned Bob and me. We did not need a doctor to show us the large tumor on the left side of my brain! The size of the tumor and swelling forced the right side of my brain over, leaving no middle line to separate left and right sides. The doctor confirmed that it was definitely cancer and needed immediate attention. He hoped sixty percent of it could be removed but my neurologist made no guarantees that I would talk or walk again, recognize my family, or even live through the operation.

The doctor's face turned white as a sheet and we sensed his concern for us. He asked if we were going to be all right, if we wanted some private time or a second opinion. I said, "I see it and I don't want it." He requested that I go home, pack a bag, and be back at the hospital within the hour. Bob and I looked at each other and said, "We will be back in an hour."

While we were gone, our daughter, Amy, said she had told Jennie, our other daughter, "I think it is cancer." Amy said tears rolled down my cheeks as I shared the news with them. Out of the mouths of babes. . . . She was way ahead of me!

As I packed, Bob made phone calls to the friends and family with whom Jesus has generously blessed us. These people are invaluable because we've all shared the ups and downs of our lives. Our friends and family all fell on their knees for me, all of us praying for healing.

> Jesus held me in the palm of his hand as I easily went to sleep singing a healing song!

By 9:00 pm, we arrived at the hospital with nurses waiting in line for my fingers, arms, and ready mouth. Our friends and family began arriving, too. Each one gave me the sense Jesus was entering the room. One friend led a heart-warming prayer that made me feel like the oil of the Holy Spirit had been poured out upon me in abundance. No value can be put on LOVE. It is an overwhelming gift beyond description I would wish for everyone who reads this story. My life has been God's, win, lose, or draw! Everyone left the hospital around midnight. I easily went to sleep because I had Jesus, my all in all, to comfort me.

Gwynel was marvelous. I remember waking up Tuesday morning and finding her on the couch. She said she couldn't sleep at home and came to the hospital in the middle of the night just to be with me. She also started a list on the first night of names of who visited, phoned, or sent flowers. I can't tell you how many times I have referred to it. Then she brought me an automatic reverse recorder with marvelous praise, worship, and healing tapes. One particular tape absolutely ministered to my spirit as only Jesus knows. I have no words to tell you the absolute faith they put in me as I learned to sing them "loudly" in my room. They were solid "I will be healed" messages from people I had never heard of that caused my Spirit to join his. They truly deepened my spiritual strength and expectation of miraculous healing.

I met my neurosurgeon, a quiet, humble man I admired, on Tuesday. He'd had difficulty getting enough time in the operating room for the Thursday surgery. So he had moved it to Wednesday! I remember surprise tears coming to my eyes because I realized the severity of my situation and that these doctors wanted to take care of me as soon as possible. Jesus held me in the palm of his hand as I easily went to sleep singing a healing song!

My parents came early on Wednesday morning, my cousins came from Longview and both took a day off from work. Everyone's concern touched me.

The doctors told me the surgery would take three and a half

hours. My neurosurgeon "woke" me up twice to answer questions and I praise God that I gave the right answers. Those answers allowed him to continue the procedure and for the surgery to last five and a half hours. He gave the results to Bob and the waiting friends. These particular cancers are graded on a scale of I (the least) to IV (the greatest). I had a Grade III Astrocytoma. The tumor was the size of a fist and it was located on top of my speech center causing my interchanging of words. The surgeon believed he had removed eighty-five to ninety percent of it.

In recovery, everyone was especially pleased that I talked and recognized people immediately. Ninety percent was far greater than my neurologist had expected! My hopes continued to be with the powerful and mighty Healer. If you grew up in a church, you'll understand why a major part of my testimony is, "The surgeon took ninety percent and the Lord got his ten percent!" What a delight to tithe the ten percent to him!

The Lord gave me the best room in ICU with a marvelous view of the Dallas skyline, which I have always loved. I felt wonderful. For the first time in SEVEN months, no HEADACHES! I had no pain in my incision area. I had a tube from the incision area to a little baby balloon to my waist for drainage. The nurses shaved off the left quarter panel of my shoulder length hair. I had a very black eye. Plus, they took off all my nail polish. I looked unique to say the least. Because my nail beds get sore, the first thing I asked Bob to bring was my nail polish! The first day in ICU I repainted my nails with my shaky hands. That's when the nurses KNEW I had had brain surgery!

After two days in ICU, the hospital moved me to a beautiful private room made for people with contagious diseases. It was as quiet as a hospital room can be, if you can ignore all the visiting nurses! The first night, another treasured friend, Diana, drove about an hour to spend the night with me. I assured her it wasn't necessary but she had already decided we needed a girl's night out. What a way to get one! She brought three unique gifts, one each for the body, soul, and spirit. Another extra special surprise was the magnificent five-dozen red and yellow rose arrangement from my darling husband!

Our Sunday school teachers who lived close to us took marvelous care of our daughters, Amy (then 14) and Jennie (then 10). They served as a phone line service between Bob and all the people who called about me. They opened their home to feed our friends. We could not have made it without them.

The surgery left forty metal stitches starting from the center of my forehead across the top of my head and down to my left ear. On the day I left the hospital, the nurse used a cute little instrument to remove half of them. Since I knew it would show up on our bill, I asked to keep it. She said "yes" when she was finished.

I spent a total of eight days in the hospital with happy doctors and nurses. I returned home on a Tuesday. My house had been cleaned, all the dirty clothes washed and folded, clean sheets put on the bed, fresh towels put in the baths, and the refrigerator filled with food. I didn't cook for a month! God and I know the names of these angels of mercy. I pray for extra jewels in their crowns for their unselfish love.

On one of my first outings I shopped for a Sunday hat, a red one, of course, because red is my favorite color. On Sunday, Bob and I went to church with me wearing a red dress and a red hat. I don't know who was the happiest me or our friends – me to see them or them to see me! From the pulpit, our Pastor said he "had seen people with hang nails miss more church than Kay did!"

I had some difficulty seeing my neurosurgeon on a post-operative appointment so they put me off for another week. I just needed my stitches removed. Remember that little tool? Bob told me *not* to remove the stitches, but I just can't wear sunglasses with them catching on the metal prong above my ear. I removed them myself with no pain at all, much to Bob's chagrin.

My medical team insisted on six weeks of radiation even with me begging not to have it, because I knew I was healed. I finally agreed. The Lord blessed me and the treatments did not make me ill. They only took fifteen minutes a day, but the radiation caused about half my hair to fall out, definitely the hardest day for me during this entire ordeal. You hope and think you are ready, but it is the PITS! I cried, then I learned to love a wig.

Now, I have no restrictions on my activities. I got MRI's about three times a year until April 1991, and most were "no change." There was a marked improvement in the size of the scar tissue. Two-thirds had gone away! Even my neurologist was excited.

I feel joy testifying to others about whose mighty hands helped my doctors and nurses. It was also a privilege to testify to my neurosurgeon. I was put on a yearly MRI schedule for ten years, but I decided seven was enough!

> I did not volunteer for brain cancer, but I got it, and Jesus has turned it into HIS glory.

I did not volunteer for brain cancer, but I got it, and Jesus has turned it into HIS glory. When people need to hear a positive story it gives me pleasure to share mine. Knowing the power of my healing Savior fills my heart with unspeakable joy. Truly, our Lord has unsearchable riches waiting for us to discover.

> *The Lord is my light and my salvation—whom shall I fear?* (Psalm 27:1)

Rejoicing Versus Sorrow

by Debby McCrary

W<small>E WERE IN AN AMAZING TIME OF OUR LIFE. E</small><small>VEN AS WE PREPARED</small> to take our precious eighteen-month-old daughter for minor surgery the next day, we had peace and confidence in the outcome. All was well. Looking back, I believe the weekly Ladies Bible Class lessons had calmed my soul. We had spent almost six weeks solely on Philippians 4:4:

> *Rejoice in the Lord always. I say it again: Rejoice! Let your gentleness be evident to all. The Lord is near. Do not be anxious about anything, but in everything, by prayer and petition, with thanksgiving, present your requests to God. And the peace of God, which transcends all understanding, will guard your hearts and your minds in Christ Jesus* (emphasis added).

As I prepared dinner, I was interrupted by a couple of phone calls. Teasingly, my husband, Marcus, said, "I don't ever get any calls; you get them all." We laughed at his comment and continued on with our evening. Within five minutes the phone rang again with a call for Marcus. I gave it to him with a smile about his previous comment.

I didn't see evidence on his side of the conversation of what was to come . . . but for me, life tumbled in, and the six weeks of "Rejoice" study fell apart. He had just gotten fired! Fired for sticking with the safety rules. Fired, because the company didn't like the cost with each "write-up." Fired for doing the right thing! So, this is how the new company that purchased the small airline worked! We had missed the previous owner, but never thought this would happen.

That night, the phone rang off the wall for Marcus. His co-workers were stunned, and they supported his decision, knowing they might be next. That night my husband held me, told me it would be all right, then said he needed to study for his college final and get some sleep. (Yes, he did both!) That night the insurance for the surgery was gone. That night, the options for the jobs he loves to do meant moving. That night I told God I could not rejoice. That night I showed him, with Bible open, all the times David cried for HIS help.

> *Away from me, all you who do evil, for the Lord has heard my weeping. The Lord has heard my cry for mercy; the Lord accepts my prayer* (Psalm 6:8-9).

That night I cried, pleading . . . "Why? How? What? God answer these questions!" HE did—in an amazing way! The doctor did the surgery free of charge. Marc's former employer gave him a job. Marc's college friend had an empty house he rented to us, a deal we couldn't turn down. Our house sold, even though we hadn't listed it "For Sale" yet. We got to live close to our nieces; they loved us, and we loved them. We reunited with friends from our dating days. That night, I didn't recall the complete rejoice Scripture in my head . . . I just questioned how I could rejoice. Now I know rejoicing comes through the prayers God answers in ways beyond me. He is my ultimate comforter and he is always beyond me!

Finding Strength in Scriptures

by Loretta Parrish

I LEARNED AT AN EARLY AGE TO LOOK FOR GOD'S HAND IN EVERYTHING and to trust him. To me, it was primary and simple: If I was afraid, I would quote the Scripture, pray, and then go on with life, confident that the solution was in process. My life has progressed with a pattern of tremendous stress and challenge followed by a period of calm. I learned to dig the well for "living water" during the calm so I would be prepared for the storm.

From age two-and-a-half to age eight-years-old, I suffered with rheumatic fever and heart problems. The doctors told my parents my heart and the huge murmur that developed would probably end my life by the age of twenty-one. However, I outgrew the fever, and, mysteriously, the murmur went away. Doctors have checked my heart and find no evidence of damage from that awful disease.

I was so glad to be healthy that I became a tomboy and a daredevil. I would climb the highest tree, swing from a tree limb over our creek and jump, jump the highest on the springboard and any other challenge that came my way. I was healthy and the future seemed bright. I gave my life to Jesus about two weeks after my eleventh birthday, and, shortly thereafter, began to teach Bible classes on Wednesday nights. I learned memory verses on Sunday mornings in my class, and also taught the small children easy verses. Little did I know, learning these verses prepared me for my new battle for survival.

> About two months before I turned twelve, we accidentally learned I had cancer.

About two months before I turned twelve, we accidentally learned I had cancer. We were in the doctor's office for my brother. My mother had had my right leg examined several months prior because of a lump on the back of the right leg, halfway between my knee and hip. It had doubled in size, so she asked the doctor to examine me. We had never even heard of cancer, but the expression on his face told us everything. As soon as surgery could be scheduled, the doctor removed a mass about the size of half of a grapefruit, leaving a scar from buttock to knee. They told me that if I lived five years without recurrence I would be cured.

About two years later during a periodic checkup, the doctor discovered the cancer had returned. He had told me earlier that it might return, but I never really thought it would, so this rattled me to my core. This time, it had changed to a more aggressive form. The surgery left a parallel scar about an inch from the first one, equally as long, and all muscle was removed from that area of my leg. I was thirteen, so physical appearance meant a lot. Now one leg was smaller than the other one and had two bright red scars. I struggled to accept the change in my body.

At this point I began to pray a lot. Every time I would get embarrassed or scared, I began to silently say the Scriptures I had memorized. My favorites included: *I can do everything through him who gives me strength* (Philippians 4:13). I repeated this many times to calm the dread and panic that seemed to just pop up unexpectedly. Then, after a deep breath, I would remember Romans 8:28: *And we know that in all things God works for the good of those who love him, who have been called according to his purpose.* Once calm, I would use my logic: I loved God. I had been called according to his purpose. So, I was certain that my Father, God, would make everything (good/bad, easy/hard, comforting/frightening) end up being for my good. It was a promise and God does not lie.

I loved Psalm 23: *The Lord is my shepherd, I shall not be in want. He makes me lie down in green pastures, he leads me beside quiet waters, he restores my soul. He guides me in paths of righteousness for his name's sake.* **Even though I walk through the valley of the shadow of death, I will fear no evil, for you are with me; your rod and your staff, they comfort me.** *You prepare a table before me in the presence of my enemies. You anoint my head with oil; my cup overflows.* **Surely goodness and love will follow me all the days of my life, and I will dwell in the house of the Lord forever** (emphasis added).

I found courage in Mark 10:27: *Jesus looked at them and said, "With man this is impossible, but not with God; all things are possible with God."*

Once again, the doctor told me that after five years with no return of the cancer, I would be cured. He taught me to do self-examinations of my leg. I was to do the exam once a week so my fingertips would be able to discern any changes under the skin. This time, I knew a recurrence was a possibility, maybe a probability, so I took the exams seriously.

About fifteen months later the cancer returned. The day my sensitive, practiced fingertips felt the deadly enemy, my whole body went cold. A dread unlike anything I had ever experienced at my young age of fourteen filled my heart. Somehow I sensed that this time would be really, really bad. I told no one what I had found. After several days of prayer, I decided to work on two things. First, I had to decide if I would be able to face my life as an amputee or if it would be better if I kept quiet and died. Second, if I decided I could live as an amputee, I had to prepare to lose my leg.

For the next week, I pondered, prayed, and visualized what I thought my life would be: school, dating, marriage, parenting, working, and all areas my immature mind visualized. I decided I could handle all of these challenges because the apostle, Paul, had said I could do everything through Christ who would give me strength, and, God would make all things work for my good. It was a promise. Satan could try and convince me Jesus did not love me, but I refused to believe him. I began to practice driving a car with my left foot. I tried hopping on one foot and standing on one foot, and soon realized I had an unusually good sense of balance. Two weeks from the day I found the new cancer, I told my parents. I could live with the help of my Lord.

> A dread unlike anything I had ever experienced at my young age of fourteen filled my heart.

This third time ended with just a biopsy because the cancer had changed to a seriously aggressive form. A week later, my parents took me to the foremost cancer surgeon in the world, in New York City. He amputated my right leg including the hip and right pelvis. That is called a hemipelvectomy and is the most extreme amputation.

The doctors said that I would never be able to use prosthesis, but I was walking four months later and still walk today. The doctors said I would not live longer than eighteen months, but it is now fifty-seven years later. The doctors said I would be unable to carry a baby since I had no bone to hold one, so I would lose them. However, my older daughter now has a son and a daughter; and, my younger daughter has a son. As you can see—God does work everything for good, and, we can do everything through the strength Jesus supplies.

God's Grace

by Jennifer Escobar

ON FEBRUARY 17, 2004, I CAME HOME EARLY AS HE WAS WALKING out the door with his bag, leaving a letter that said:

> I'm leaving. I can't do it anymore. I'm not in love with you, and I don't want to be with you. I don't want to preach. I don't want to do mission work. I don't want any of it at all. I realize I'm turning my back on a lot of people, but that's ok. I know this will be a big shock to you, but perhaps it isn't. I've been having an affair for the past three months. There is no way back for us, no way at all. Regardless of who you get to try and talk to me it isn't going to work, so I wouldn't even bother. In saying that I want a divorce. I have left you some money for now and I will be paying child support when we get all that figured out. I will not abandon the girls; I love them dearly, and want to see them. I just can't stay here and pretend everything is ok when it is not and it never will be. That's all I've got.

The trauma of this day and the divorce that followed catapulted many of my unhealthy tendencies into unmanageable hurts, hang ups, and habits. My need to control went defiantly out of control in every area. I have heard perfectionism described as "insecurity as an art form" which describes my life for several years and even now sometimes.

I tried to control everything and everyone around me. If someone made a mistake at work I would spend hours researching to show it was not my fault (even though my boss did not even care about the mistake). I had a truth-without-grace mentality when dealing with student workers at both my jobs on campus that put me in positions of authority. I got straight A's at the expense of time with my kids, and when I reflect on graduating *cum laude* it is not a simple sense of accomplishment.

A lot of what I did was about perfectionism to me and it represents time lost with my kids that I will never get back. I also quickly took on "victim" and "no wrong doer" mentalities. I worked two and sometimes three jobs to be the single mother martyr, my house had to be perfect, and I thought I had to be perfect and look perfect. I thought at first that if I lost weight he would come back, so I went to Weight Watchers and started working out (which sounds like a good thing). However, I developed an unhealthy need to control my diet. One day I was working at the cafeteria at the university I attended and someone came and introduced himself to me and said "You're Jen? You're not fat and ugly. I heard you were fat and ugly and that is why your husband left." I felt like someone said out loud all of my thoughts, and panic set in. Starting then, and for six years after, anytime I ate too much I purged my body.

I began attending Celebrate Recovery, a support group at my church, four years ago. I learned I was in DEEP denial about my eating disorder and overspending. I did not think I had any "outward" addictions, but God began to peel back the layers like an onion and showed me what I needed to work on when I was ready to work on it.

My life is SOOO different now. In a testimony I once heard, "It is in your greatest tragedy that your ministry usually lies." I have felt a call to foreign missions since I was a young girl, and ever since I stepped off the mission field twelve years ago I have felt a hole in my life. Since I joined the ministry team at my church as the female encourager that hole has been filled. I find great joy being a part of a "misfit and struggler" team again. It is so encouraging to witness God healing and working in broken lives. I no longer feel like the verse in James that talks about "being a double-minded man unstable in all he does." I no longer feel the need to fix the hurt in my children due to the divorce, because the hurt is not mine to fix. It is their journey and my only job is to love them along the way. It is God's hurt to fix in them and their journey to allow him to do so. I am a much better boss and co-worker because I am able to see the gray areas most of life resides in. I can apologize when I am wrong and look for opportunities to make amends. I have a quiet time with God every day and can pray now.

> I had believed the false church message "God is good. You're bad. Try harder."

I can sit and listen to someone with the intent of supporting, without the compulsion to fix them or their struggle. My recovery has been a journey filled with peaks and pits. I relapsed with my compulsive overspending, once with my eating disorder, and frequently with my depression that comes out as anger, but now I do not let depression deepen or shame overrun my life. As a wise person said, "I am still someone who struggles, but struggles well and with hope."

God, through Celebrate Recovery, brought me to a place of peace and true forgiveness with my divorce and he helped me put my ex-husband back in human skin. I truly learned that "hurt people, hurt people." Bible study brought me to a place of compassion and the inventory process for me was one of the hardest but the most beautiful transformations. Writing out everything I had done and everything done to me helped me come out of self-righteousness and a judgmental spirit and made me embrace the idea of humility. I have since heard, "Until you have experienced grace you cannot be gracious." I was blocking God's grace in my life with shame and unworthiness. I had believed the false church message "God is good. You're bad. Try harder." And once I finally accepted and embraced grace, God started me on a journey of forgiveness. Forgiveness for me is defined as: "Giving up the hope that the past could have been any different."

So, I write all of this to say what I believe that all of life boils down to fulfilling the Bible verse that follows. It is what really matters when it is all said and done. It has and continues to be a daily and life goal, and I have this verse hanging on my wall at work and in my home: *And what does the LORD require of you? To act justly and to love mercy and to walk humbly with your God* (Micah 6:8).

For My Fellow Worriers

by Tina Ware-Walters, PhD

> *Cast all your anxiety on him because he cares for you (1 Peter 5:7).*

WHEN WE STARTED THE MOUNTAIN OF PAPERWORK REQUIRED for Adoption approval I thought my husband, Matt, and I, would feel elated when we completed it, and that the part that followed, our wait for a baby, would be blissful and easy. I was partially right. When we turned in our finished packet after months of work, we felt happy and a huge step closer to parenthood. Thinking we could get a baby any day thrilled me! However, I was wrong to think I would find the next part—the waiting—easy.

Once we got to the waiting stage of the adoption process we had all sorts of newfound free time. Matt made use of the extra hours by working in the yard, watching movies, reading books, and relaxing. Unfortunately, as the weeks turned into months, I began to use my free time less constructively. We had wanted a baby for a long time and I let impatience get the best of me. I checked our agency's web page daily, which is not a bad or unusual thing for prospective parents to do, but I looked sometimes several times a day, almost willing a baby to pop out through the computer screen. And, worse, I thought up concerns about our adoption and why a birth mother hadn't chosen us yet or might not choose us. I wondered if being in our early 40s made us too old, or if the fact that our future child would not have a stay-at-home-parent, or if us being childless would keep us from getting picked. When a family from our agency would get chosen, while I cheered for them, I would also wonder what made them more desirable than us. All of my worries seemed valid, but thinking about them constantly was pretty useless and counter-productive, and made the wait seem longer.

> All of my worries seemed valid, but thinking about them constantly was pretty useless and counter-productive, and made the wait seem longer.

About a month ago I read in my daily devotional book a lesson that included 1 Peter 5:7. The verse spoke to me and I immediately memorized it. I felt like God had included it in the Bible for the expert worriers, like me. The words "Cast ALL (emphasis mine) your anxiety on him" brought me an instant sense of peace. Suddenly, all of the factors that might impede our getting a child seemed to melt away. I sensed God saying, "Give your concerns to me. I love you and I will take care of you, like I always do." Meditating on the words of 1 Peter 5:7 made me feel closer to God and calmer about our adoption situation, in addition to other concerns I encountered.

Since I have focused on giving my concerns to God, our agency has placed two babies with families much younger than Matt and me, families with kids and stay-at-home moms. Basically, I have seen my adoption fears realized. Sure, I have felt a twinge of jealousy. But, then I have repeated 1 Peter 5:7, and God has replaced my jealousy with excitement for these families and their new children, and he has blessed me with peace about our situation, and hope about the baby that will join our family one day.

The Healing Power of God's Word

by Jolene Schmidt

> *Finally, brothers, whatever is true, whatever is noble, whatever is right, whatever is pure, whatever is lovely, whatever is admirable—if anything is excellent or praiseworthy—think about such things* (Philippians 4:8).

In August 1992 I accepted a teaching position. I had taught before having our children, Gabriel and Bethany. While they were young I chose to stay home. I stayed busy with home, church, and school activities.

I received the teaching position when Gabriel was in the third grade and Bethany was in the first. Taking the job seemed like a good idea. It was an overflow combination class of second and third graders, and I later found out the children were ones no one else wanted, and that the school never used the overflow classroom again.

I took the job on a Wednesday and converted a storage room into a classroom. I needed help: books, desks, chairs, a chalkboard, decorations, and curriculum school supplies. Something deep stirred in me, but I just dismissed it and kept on going as I put my classroom in order.

As I made arrangements for our children I felt a little bit of guilt. I had always been there for them. However, with them in school full-time I had a lot of free time on my hands. I had always loved teaching and this job seemed to be the answer.

Monday arrived and I greeted my students with a smile and a soft hug. I wanted them to feel safe and relaxed. As the days went by, I found myself getting up earlier and staying later at school. I also started to lose weight and my sleep pattern changed. As a perfectionist I tried to be the super mom, super wife, super Christian, super friend, and super teacher.

> As a perfectionist I tried to be the super mom, super wife, super Christian, super friend, and super teacher.

My teaching went well but class preparations tired me and I had a hard time separating second and third grade lessons. I wondered how in the world my grandmother had taught in a one-room schoolhouse.

I had family and friends giving me advice and encouragement. Even the superintendent came in and helped me, but then a few other teachers would come in, always stressed out about how my class would affect the test scores at the end of the school year.

By the end of the first nine weeks I had lost twenty pounds and I was not sleeping well. The school gave me a student teacher at the end of the first nine weeks. She was wonderful, young, and beautiful inside and out. I told her this class would be hers at the end of

December. She resisted, but I insisted.

I resigned at the end of December, and I thought I would get better. I still slept very little and continued to lose weight. I felt like a failure and entered a dark fog.

Glen, my husband of seventeen years, and I didn't realize it, but I was going into a deep depression, something unfamiliar to us. Glen suggested everything he could think of to help me: sleeping pills, hot toddies, exercise, hot baths, soft music, massages, etc.

Eventually, my depression became so bad that I went for thirty days to a Christian-based hospital that specializes in depression. This began a long journey of mental hospitals, medications, manic episodes, and therapy sessions. Through fifteen years of treatment, I learned I had repressed a childhood trauma. I was diagnosed bipolar with PTSD (post-traumatic stress disorder) panic attacks.

One of my first therapists reassured me I was not crazy. "You are not crazy when you lose six months of sleep and suffer an extreme amount of weight loss and stress. Your mind is just stressed and sick," was the message I received. One of the best pieces of advice the doctor gave me was to memorize a Bible verse and to recite it daily, morning and evening. This Scripture has comforted me and kept me moving forward in this journey, one step at a time. The verse is Philippians 4:8: *Finally, brothers, whatever is true, whatever is noble, whatever is right, whatever is pure, whatever is lovely, whatever is admirable—if anything is excellent or praiseworthy—think about such things.*

Today I am fifty-five years old and I live a full and happy life, with some ups and downs. I keep my life as tranquil as possible. I use my tools: prayer, meditation, journaling, Scripture reading, exercise, healthy eating habits, positive thinking, medications, therapy sessions, and play. My husband and children are still my greatest supporters, along with some family members. And, we all lean on the Lord and his people for understanding, as we did even when we didn't understand what was happening to me. God's hand was and is on my family.

My story is ongoing and has helped others dealing with mental illness issues. I feel blessed. Philippians 4:8 keeps me in tune to what God wants for me. I still daily recite Philippians 4:8, morning and evening.

Our Little Fisherman

by Jacci Gantz

> We have this hope as an anchor for the soul, firm and secure (Hebrews 6:19).

O<small>N A FREEZING, RAINY WINTER DAY,</small> I <small>WAS HEADING TO THE DOCTOR'S</small> office for my weekly fertility treatment, driving by three-foot snow drifts. My car began sliding into oncoming traffic on the black ice, and barely missed plowing down an icy embankment. My vehicle finally stopped sliding sideways. In tears I frantically cried out to God, "What am I doing? This doctor's visit will be just like the previous five visits: more shots and more medication and those conciliatory doctor's words—'I am sorry; you are not pregnant this time.'"

Before he could respond to my question, I answered myself: "I'm doing everything possible to become pregnant." God's calm voice then spoke to me from Hebrews 6:19. He assured me of his love, wrapped comforting arms around my mind, and let me know I was not less of a woman because I could not become pregnant. I was not a failure. In the epiphany of the moment, I turned the car toward home. Arriving home, I told my husband I was tired of being a doctor's experiment and that we should adopt. I had such a peace about me that my husband immediately agreed.

> I told my husband I was tired of being a doctor's experiment and that we should adopt. I had such a peace about me that my husband immediately agreed.

With the extensive paperwork finished, more doctors' appointments made, and recommendations given, we lived in a glass house for months. Psychological testing, home studies, unscheduled visits, the list was endless. We were informed that at any time during the process, we could be denied and never learn why. Walking on eggshells is nerve-wracking. Needless to say, my husband was astonished that I had such peace about me. I kept telling him that God had a baby for us. He would ask me how I knew and I would say, "He told me so." My husband was in total agreement, but still worried about me. Like Mary and Sarah in the Bible, I had had a dream that God was preparing a baby for us. Nothing could convince me otherwise. I was resting in God's peace through Hebrews 6:19.

Months marched by. No news. Then one day I got the phone call at work: A baby boy was ours if we wanted him. My first thought was, "Are you crazy! Yes, we want him." But a quiet voice kept telling me, "This is not the one." I cried, trying to convince God that this was my baby, but after hours of prayer and frantic phone calls with my husband, God's quiet voice was still telling me this baby was not ours. I accepted God's will and again I was surprisingly at peace.

About a month later close friends asked us to go camping with them, but I informed them we could not leave town because God was giving us a baby. They just patronizingly shook their heads at me while mouthing to my husband, "Is she going to be okay?"

Two weeks later, THE phone call came. When I answered, the adoption supervisor asked if we had an extra fishing pole because I had told her we might spend a weekend at the lake. I said that we indeed did have extra fishing poles. She then told us we had a beautiful brown-haired, brown-eyed baby boy waiting to take him fishing.

When the nurse put our baby in my arms, God spoke to me and said, "This is the one. He will be a fisherman of men." God gave me strength in a seemingly impossible situation. After years of heartache, our boy was home.

PERSPECTIVE

It's so easy for us to become self-absorbed and to concentrate on our problems, which are often rather insignificant, instead of opening our eyes to God's rich blessings. We also tend to focus on others' shortcomings instead our own. Or, we become so consumed with guilt about our sin that we forget about God's grace and forgiveness. This section of *Our Favorite Verses* is designed to help you re-think the way you live and view your life.

In the "Perspective" section the authors gently prompt us to evaluate our thoughts and actions. They include lessons that push us to think past our troubles and notice God's blessings instead. The essay entitled "Attitude Adjustment" challenges us to realize that many of our difficulties are simply "first world" problems, and the author introduces us to the cure for "chronic complaining." "Can You Spare a Dollar?" dares you to live a life of gratitude versus one of greed. "Relaxing in Grace" reminds us to rest in God's grace because it is a gift from him. All of the stories will nudge you toward a deeper sense of peace and joy.

Attitude Adjustment

by James D. Dvorak

W E LIVE IN A CULTURE OF CHRONIC COMPLAINING AND FAULT-finding. In fact, not only does our culture merely tolerate complaining, it actually *breeds* it and provides it with an environment in which it can grow and thrive. An interesting genre is developing on the major social networking sites on the Internet that challenges chronic complainers by poking fun—usually with sarcasm and/or biting irony—at the kinds of complaints people are posting. Many of these retorts, generally tagged with the moniker "first world problems" (or FWP), are, quite frankly, down-right funny; others are not so funny; still others are the furthest thing from humorous and sometimes shockingly disturbing. The following three examples, ranging from fairly innocent to mildly shocking, were found with Google, searching the keyword "first world problems complaints."

> *It's 74 degrees and sunny, and I can't decide if I should use the air conditioner or open the car windows.*

> *I just got back from a boring trip my Dad made me take for Spring Break. I was like, "Dad, I've been to*

the Bahamas like a bajillion times! Can't I go to Mexico this year?!?" And he just said "No" and made me go on a cruise.

[From a mother to her daughter's daycare provider] *Today we were in the store and [my daughter] pointed out the type of cookies you served at the teddy bear picnic. Much to my dismay, they weren't a name brand. My husband and I pay very good money for childcare and we expect corners won't be cut in the care of our child. That and we don't want to instill the sorts of values in her that make her think it's okay to settle for less than the best. That might be hard for you to understand, but it means a lot to me.*

> It's 74 degrees and sunny, and I can't decide if I should use the air conditioner or open the car windows.

Some will read these examples as humorous, others as shockingly horrible, but no matter how you read them they underscore the point that people—no, *I*—complain way too much! What's more, these examples betray the fact that often my complaints are about things that ultimately don't really matter much if at all! So, I find I am often in need of an attitude adjustment—one in which my sad, self-pitying attitude of complaint and faultfinding is replaced with a strong sense of *gratitude*. For a life that abides in Christ and in which Christ abides is a life of gratitude.

One must be careful not to confuse gratitude with happiness. Generally speaking, happiness is based on happenstance; that is, one may or may not experience happiness depending on what she or he may experience from one moment to the next. Gratitude, on the other hand, is more than a feeling. It is a discipline. Henri Nouwen, one of the twentieth century's most beloved pastoral theologians, writes:

> *In the past I always thought of gratitude as a spontaneous response to the awareness of gifts received, but now I realise [sic] gratitude can also be lived as a discipline. **The discipline of gratitude is the explicit effort to acknowledge that all I am and have is given to me as a gift of love, a gift to be celebrated with joy.** . . . Gratitude as a discipline involves a conscious choice. **I can choose to be grateful even when my emotions and feelings are still steeped in hurt and resentment.** It is amazing how many occasions present themselves in which I can choose gratitude instead of a complaint. I can choose to be grateful when I am criticized [sic], even when my heart still responds in bitterness. I can choose to speak about goodness and beauty, even when my inner eye still looks for someone to accuse or something to call ugly. I can choose to listen to the voices that forgive and to look at the faces that smile, even while I still hear words of revenge and see grimaces of hatred* (emphasis added).[3]

New Testament scholar David Garland makes the excellent point that "true Christians experience God's grace intensely and allow their gratitude for what God has done in Christ to shape their whole life," and that "this gratitude makes life richer, happier, and more wondrous."[4] More importantly, the Bible calls believers to lives characterized by thankfulness and thanksgiving (see, for example, 1 Thessalonians 5:16–18; Philippians 4:4–7).

The antidote for chronic complaining, then, is a healthy dose of gratitude. There are a number of ways by which a person can adjust her or his attitude from one of complaint to one of gratitude. Taking a cue from Nouwen, one way is to engage in *worship*. I am not referring here to the ways we typically define worship, which, frankly, is typically more self-centered than God-focused. Rather, by "worship," I mean engaging in an *intentional and intense focus upon God and the gracious act of redemption he worked on our behalf*—or, in Nouwen's words quoted already, "the explicit effort to acknowledge that all I am given and have is given to me as a gift of love, a gift to be celebrated with joy." In those moments of my own life when I need an attitude adjustment, I practice intentional, intense focus on God and what he accomplished for me by turning to a specific text in the Scriptures, Psalm 103:1-13. I recommend reading the entire psalm, but the first thirteen verses are especially important. I quote them here from the NRSV:

> *Bless the Lord, O my soul, and all that is within me, bless his holy name. Bless the Lord, O my soul, and do not forget all his benefits—who forgives all your iniquity, who heals all your diseases, who redeems your life from the Pit, who crowns you with steadfast love and mercy, who satisfies you with good as long as you live so that your youth is renewed like the eagle's.*
>
> *The Lord works vindication and justice for all who are oppressed. He made known his ways to Moses, his acts to the people of Israel. The Lord is merciful and gracious, slow to anger and abounding in steadfast love. He will not always accuse, nor will he keep his anger forever.*
>
> *He does not deal with us according to our sins, nor repay us according to our iniquities. For as the heavens are high above the earth, so great is his steadfast*

> *love toward those who fear him; as far as the east is from the west, so far he removes our transgressions from us. As a father has compassion for his children, so the Lord has compassion for those who fear him.*

This psalm, clearly a psalm of praise (although it is one likely rehearsed in both good times and tough times, is structured in such a way that God's beneficent actions toward his people are emphasized. The psalmist opens the piece with a charge to his soul/innermost being to *bless the Lord*. He immediately follows this with a host of reasons why the Lord is to be blessed, namely because of "all his benefits." He:

- forgives all our iniquities
- heals our diseases
- redeems our lives from "the Pit"
- crowns us with steadfast love and mercy
- satisfies us with good so that our youth is renewed like the eagle's
- works vindication and justice for those of us who are oppressed
- does not deal with us as our sins deserve, but removes our transgressions from us
- keeps his covenant with those who respect him.

One reason this text is among my favorite verses is that it speaks so clearly and forcefully about God's grace and mercy, and it focuses our hearts on the fact that *all we are and have is given to us as a gift of love, a gift to be celebrated with joy.* This focus helps us overcome complaining with *gratitude*.

Buddy, Can You Spare a Dollar?

by Tim Dallas

I'M ABOUT TO LEAVE A CHURCH WHERE MY KIDS PRACTICE BASKETBALL when a man walks into the foyer of the church and asks me for two quarters or a dollar for gas. He adds that a church is a place where people find help. I'm not sure I believe he needs money for gas exactly, but I know I'll feel guilty if I don't help so I reach into my wallet and fish out a $5 bill thinking the man will be excited since his high request was $1. He takes the $5 and then asks if he can have another $5. I give him an incredulous look as I put my wallet back in my pocket. He takes the "you're pressing your luck" hint, shakes my hand, thanks me, and leaves.

At first I am a little miffed at him, but then I realize he is a picture of how I respond to God sometimes. I pray for blessings for family, friends, and for me and God faithfully answers. Yet, I can receive and witness these blessings and still ask God . . . "Is that it? Why

> He takes the $5 and then asks if he can have another $5.

didn't I get the bonus set of steak knives with my order?" Having a mindset of gratefulness goes a long way toward contentment, which is where Jesus wants us to exist.

> *For this reason I bow my knees before the Father, from whom every family in heaven and on earth derives its name, that He would grant you, according to the riches of His glory, to be strengthened with power through His Spirit in the inner man, so that Christ may dwell in your hearts through faith; and that you, being rooted and grounded in love, may be able to comprehend with all the saints what is the breadth and length and height and depth, and to know the love of Christ which surpasses knowledge, that you may be filled up to all the fullness of God. Now to Him who is able to do far more abundantly beyond all that we ask or think, according to the power that works within us, to Him be the glory in the church and in Christ Jesus to all generations, forever and ever. Amen* (Ephesians 3:14-21, NASB).

How Has God Been Good to You This Week?

by Sarah Hinds

THE PAST FEW YEARS OF MY LIFE HAVE BEEN CHALLENGING IN MANY ways, and often I am tempted to look back on my struggles, get discouraged, and wonder why things have turned out the way they have. After all, in an ideal world, all would be perfect and those who worked hard would be able to enjoy the fruits of their labor. Of course, this isn't such a world and recent events have reminded me of this stark reality.

Not too long ago, I was directed to Psalm 73, a passage in which the writer explores why the godly suffer so frequently. It has since helped to sustain me, as the chapter's theme seems to be this: life is not fair, but God is good. The psalm begins by proving the unfairness of life. Midway through the psalm, though, there is a turning point when the writer brings himself into the presence of God and places his frustrations before him. In doing this, the man's focus shifts and God responds by continually lifting him up. *My flesh and my heart may fail*, the psalmist says, **but God is the strength of my heart and my portion forever** (verse 26, emphasis added).

One of the blessings I've experienced since being a part of my current church home is the moment each Sunday when the ques-

> One of the blessings I've experienced since being a part of my current church home is the moment each Sunday when the question is raised, "How has God been good to you this week?"

tion is raised, "How has God been good to you this week?" For me, this is a time when life gets put back in perspective. It's a reminder that blessings can be found in every trial and that, ultimately, *God causes all things to work together for good to those who love him* (see Romans 8:28, NASB). While we see the pain or sorrow, we also see the goodness. Remembering God has favored me—just as he did Israel—reassures me as I hold on to his grace and mercy.

Life is surely not fair. Yet, God is so good and he is faithful to his children. Even at our lowest moments, God is still God. His comfort and assurance sustain me as I come into his presence and lay my frustrations at his feet so he can shift my focus. I gain perspective and am thankful for his goodness.

> *Surely God is good to Israel, to those who are pure in heart. But as for me, my feet had almost slipped; I had nearly lost my foothold. For I envied the arrogant when I saw the prosperity of the wicked. They have no struggles; their bodies are healthy and strong. They are free from the burdens common to man; they are not plagued by human ills. Therefore pride is their necklace; they clothe themselves with violence. From their callous hearts comes iniquity; the evil conceits of their minds know no limits. They scoff, and speak*

with malice; in their arrogance they threaten oppression. Their mouths lay claim to heaven, and their tongues take possession of the earth. Therefore their people turn to them and drink up waters in abundance. They say, "How can God know? Does the Most High have knowledge?" This is what the wicked are like—always carefree, they increase in wealth.

Surely in vain have I kept my heart pure; in vain have I washed my hands in innocence. All day long I have been plagued; I have been punished every morning. If I had said, "I will speak thus," I would have betrayed your children. When I tried to understand all this, it was oppressive to me till I entered the sanctuary of God; then I understood their final destiny. Surely you place them on slippery ground; you cast them down to ruin. How suddenly are they destroyed, completely swept away by terrors! As a dream when one awakes, so when you arise, O Lord, you will despise them as fantasies.

When my heart was grieved and my spirit embittered, I was senseless and ignorant; I was a brute beast before you. Yet I am always with you; you hold me by my right hand. You guide me with your counsel, and afterward you will take me into glory. Whom have I in heaven but you? And earth has nothing I desire besides you. My flesh and my heart may fail, but God is the strength of my heart and my portion forever. Those who are far from you will perish; you destroy all who are unfaithful to you. But as for me, it is good to be near God. I have made the Sovereign LORD my refuge; I will tell of all your deeds (Psalm 73).

Hope From Forgiveness

by Gina Simpson

Before I became a Christian I was plagued with guilt. I had sin in my life and felt that even God couldn't forgive me, but the following passage made me realize that God can forgive anything and anyone:

> *Do you not know that the wicked will not inherit the kingdom of God? Do not be deceived: Neither the sexually immoral nor idolaters nor adulterers nor male prostitutes nor homosexual offenders nor thieves nor the greedy nor drunkards nor slanderers, nor swindlers will inherit the kingdom of God. And that is what some of you were. But you were washed, you were sanctified, you were justified in the name of the Lord Jesus Christ and by the Spirit of our God* (1 Corinthians 6:9-11).

This passage also gives me hope that, even in these times when sin is readily accepted by society, I can share God's Word with anyone. Everyone has the opportunity to be obedient and gain forgiveness and salvation.

> I always tell the girls we can never go back and change what has happened, but there remains the opportunity to get on "the straight and narrow."

My experience is that when people first hear the gospel they feel the weight of sin in their lives. With the teen girls I teach, I see premarital sex, drinking, and drugs most frequently. Some of them worry they are "too bad" to be forgiven. Lots of people are under the illusion they took the wrong path and now they are trapped and stuck. My favorite verses represent the chance to get back on the right path.

I always tell the girls we can never go back and change what has happened, but there remains the opportunity to get on "the straight and narrow." God gives us all the option to repent, confess Jesus as Christ, and to have our sins forgiven. Just like those in Corinth we can get on the right path. Then we must remember we are a different person. We don't forget the things we were or what we have done, but we are new and starting from that point we live our lives differently. I love to witness the hope these verses give those who feel so lost in their sin, and I especially love when they do repent and follow the steps the Bible sets forth for salvation.

Relaxing in Grace

by Charles Rix, PhD

> *Do not be overrighteous, neither be overwise—why destroy yourself?* (Ecclesiastes 7:16).
>
> *But he said to me, "My grace is sufficient for you, for my power is made perfect in weakness"* (2 Corinthians 12:9).

As a young pianist, I learned Franz Liszt's Paganini Étude "La Campanella" before I knew the meaning of the word "fear." The mental and physical gymnastics of the piece were intoxicating to play and the sensation of performing the piece was somewhat akin to bungee jumping off a bridge. As a developing classical pianist, the drive to conquer the "dare-devil" pyrotechnics of the Chopin Études, the Schumann, Ravel, or Prokofiev Toccatas or daring to attempt the dangers of the Brahms Paganini Études kept me occupied for hours on end. I sought any opportunity to practice so I could perform these brain-bending pieces as perfectly as possible.

It was once said that a basketball player making ninety percent of his or her shots would be considered a very good player, while a concert pianist achieving only ninety percent accuracy in a performance would be considered a dismal failure. I did not want to fail, and I practiced to be sure that when I walked out on stage I would avoid disaster and succeed. There was no performance by a visiting pianist, no available recording, and no master class by a resident artist at a local university that I did not press into the service of my musical and technical development.

However, as I got older and began to juggle demands on my time and energy between practice, performance, "income-producing-work," ministry, and raising a family, the thrill of slaying the dragons of the piano literature turned to trepidation. Without adequate opportunity to fully work out the technical and musical aspects of the pieces I enjoyed, I no longer felt as secure or as confident to simply walk out on stage and toss off one of these knuckle-breakers as if it were child's play. Sitting down to give a full-length recital, salt and peppered with these piano dazzlers, was accompanied by shaking knees, trembling, and a lot of second-guessing. Would I be able to actually execute the leaps on the last two pages of the Prokofiev Seventh Sonata without cracking the top notes? Would my repeated note technique work as quickly as it should in the Ravel Toccata or Liszt's La Campanella? Would my memory hold up in the second movement of the Bach Italian Concerto? Without staying close to these pieces that were once second nature, revisiting them only occasionally felt like seeing friends who had moved away. It took a while to remember how I used to "converse" with them.

Yikes.

In my youth, I did not have these questions, or these doubts, or this . . . fear.

I've always threatened to write a book entitled, "Everything I Know about Life, I Learned at the Piano." In many ways, work at the piano has been one of my greatest teachers. Almost every emotion and life experience is scored and experienced through working on the vast array of pieces in the piano repertoire. Now, in these difficult passages—of which there are no end—fear, doubt, and insecurities, became like uninvited guests loitering around the piano bench. They taunted and teased me as I battled my way through finger tangling passages to get the phrasing right. Fighting the fear of not being able to play the piece, bucking doubt I had the ability to succeed, and resisting the insecurities that I wasn't as good as the next pianist were the ingredients for many hours of practice—*unproductive* practice that is—that left me exhausted, discouraged, and not wanting to play for anyone.

A very good friend of mine had literally ruined his right hand trying to slay the difficulties of Liszt's Dante Sonata only to give up the piano entirely for a career in computer programming. For years, he refused to touch the piano. A tale too often told. But I kept practicing because I was not going to be that person.

But thankfully I discovered another way from a very wise teacher I engaged while I was working on my graduate degree. I was introduced to this new way during a lesson on Ravel's "Jeux d'eau," my favorite piece of piano music but with an ending that is like walking the high wire with no safety net below.

Terrifying.

This very wise teacher taught me how to "relax into music," so I could walk this high wire and not fall. Ravel, a brilliant French impressionistic composer, but not a very good pianist, wrote some of the most exquisite music for the piano but that required the most awkward hand positions. During this first lesson on the "Jeux d'eau," my teacher listened for a while even while noticing the tension in my arms and hands. He asked why I had such difficulty playing some of the passages. I responded with a long explanation of all the things I had tried for years to execute without success. I had read every book, sought help from every pianist I met, and practiced for hours, only to remain frustrated and defeated.

He stopped me in my anxious explanations and asked me to just relax. He carefully placed my hands in one particularly difficult position. Then, he instructed me to just sit at the piano until I accepted the feeling of awkwardness. I remember sitting there in silence for some time. He requested me to play the passage and not think about the hand position, but listen to the music. For the first time, I understood it was precisely the unusual feeling in the hand that was integral to the production of this beautiful music.

From this "aha" moment, I learned my technical problems were largely musical problems. Accepting the physical sensation made it possible to hear the music and allow the music to come forth and carry me through the piece. Learning to "relax in the music" freed my hands to do what they needed to do to play the piece. No longer did the discomfort dominate my thinking. Rather, the music became uppermost in my mind. The difficulties of the piece remained, but my hands simply glided through them with much greater ease.

> For me, trusting the sufficiency of God's grace begins with recognizing that I cannot fix what is not "fixable" and to receive God's ability and peace to meet the challenges of the situation.

A piano lesson, yes, but also a spiritual lesson, and a *life* lesson. How often I have tried to "conquer" the difficulties in my life, "be good," and "get it right," only to become discouraged when things did not go perfectly. How long I have sought to be "overwise," only to feel dehumanized, demoralized, or even destroyed, when my "goodness," "righteousness," or "wisdom" either didn't measure up to what was needed, or simply did not work in a particular difficult situation. How many difficult passages in my own life I have tried to "fix" through either fighting them, or "trying harder," only to realize in the end what the writer of Ecclesiastes knew all along, "What is crooked cannot be made straight." How many times I have nearly destroyed myself trying to be "overrighteous" when what I really needed to do was to accept the difficulty, and listen to the music of God, "My grace is sufficient for you."

There have been so many instances in my life—more than I care to count—when I have run up against situations that were not "fixable." The untimely deaths of my sister and my wife from cancer, ministry situations where dealing with difficult congregants was simply over my head, financial reversals resulting from the economy, and friends that turned out to be "not friends" are only a few examples. Yet dealing with each of these situations is like learning to execute a difficult passage of piano music. Moving through difficulty requires not fighting the situation with anxiety but rather *relaxing into the music* of the situation, God's sufficient grace.

For me, trusting the sufficiency of God's grace begins with recognizing that I cannot fix what is not "fixable" and to receive God's ability and peace to meet the challenges of the situation. I cannot straighten that which is crooked. Like many passages at the piano that will forever remain wickedly difficult, life will continue to dole out situations for which there is no satisfactory solution. But the wisdom of Ecclesiastes and the encouragement of the Lord through the apostle Paul cohere with life lessons at the piano. I could destroy myself by trying to be "too good," trying to be "too wise," and trying too hard to "get it right." Rather, if I accept the feeling of awkwardness of what comes my way and relax in God's sufficient ability to carry me through these moments of "impossibility," I will be able to play the life God has granted.

Is That Our Church?

by Gina Simpson

> *But in your hearts set apart Christ as Lord. Always be prepared to give an answer to everyone who asks you to give the reason for the hope that you have* (1 Peter 3:15).

IN A RECENT GOSPEL MEETING AT CHURCH OUR PASTOR PRESENTED lessons on following in the footprints of Jesus. He spoke about the steps of Jesus leading to his church and explained that the church isn't "our" church but Christ's.

I was impressed with how well the children behaved each night and this morning I found out they were listening as well. I have several devotional songs I'm trying to learn and found YouTube videos of church congregations singing them. This morning I was playing a new song and my son, Isaac, came up and looked at the iPod and said, "Is that our church?" So I took the opportunity and asked him, "Whose church is it?" and he said, "God's." Then I asked him, "Who bought the church?" and he said, "Jesus." So far he'd been following the preacher's outline, so I followed up with "How did Jesus pay for the church?" and Isaac said "He had to die. That's sad." We talked a little more and Isaac came to the conclusion, "Jesus died so we could be members of his church and go to heaven."

> So I took the opportunity and asked him, "Whose church is it?" and he said, "God's."

We recently had a youth day and I had the opportunity to speak to the young ladies about being ready to give and answer from 1 Peter 3:15. In the lesson I talked a little about earning money versus being given money to spend. I've noticed with my kids if they want something and I tell them they can do chores to earn the money to buy it, once they've earned the money sometimes they decide to save it instead of spending it.

Adults can be similar. Doesn't bonus money usually go faster than our weekly paycheck? Do we tend to order more food when someone else is taking us out to eat versus what we would order if we were paying for our meal ourselves? What if we had to donate blood to earn money? What if stores had blood bank lines and when you took your new shoes up to the counter instead of getting out your wallet you sat in a chair, a nurse put a needle in your arm, and you had to give a pint of blood, or a quart, or a gallon? How long would most of us wait to get new shoes?

Jesus didn't give a little blood for the church; he gave all of it! I find it highly contradictory when people say they love Jesus but not his church. If we love Jesus we'll love the things he loves, and what does he love more than the one thing he gave his life for? He gave his life for the assembly, the congregation, the called out people, *his* church!

Search Inside First

by Berlin Fang

Why do you look at the speck of sawdust in your brother's eye and pay no attention to the plank in your own eye? (Matthew 7:3).

I LOVE DRINKING HOT GREEN TEA, AND I ALWAYS BRING A LARGE bottle of tea to work. Green tea is such a delicate thing that a bad container may spoil the flavor or lose the heat. I found a bottle that is just right for keeping both the temperature and the flavor. However, this bottle has an intricate opening that involves a spout, a button, a rubber spout stopper and a transparent plastic cover. It is such a complex bottle that I imagine I ought to get an engineering degree to use it.

One day, I brought it to work. I pressed the button expecting the opening apparatus to work, but the transparent lid was so tight I had to open it manually, which I did. The lid finally opened and I heard a popping sound. I must have blinked and when I looked at it again the rubber stopper was gone. Probably due to the difference in air pressure in and outside the bottle, the stopper just shot off. I searched under my desk, behind my file cabinets and on top of my bookshelves. I simply couldn't find it. It was a mystery. That thing just vanished into some kind of a black hole in the universe.

Later that day, I came home and went to the sink to wash the bottle, or what remained of it, and the rubber piece fell out. It became clear only then that it had fallen inside my bottle. I just wasted time looking outside.

> The Chinese have a saying: "Sweep the snow in front of your own door, and ignore the frost on others' roofs."

This came like an epiphany to me. This weird little incident seemed to suggest that we should look inside first when there is a problem. We seem to have an instinct to search outside first for something to blame when a problem comes up. People do this, and countries do this as well. Turn on the TV and you will notice that the season for the blame game never ends. It seems difficult to keep having issues with ourselves. We search instead for things outside to blame.

When we encounter a potential issue, we ought to ask first: are we going to be liable ourselves? When buying car insurance in some states, car owners often buy both liability and comprehensive coverage, covering potential risk for their own cars and those of others. In other states, car owners only insure their own cars, which might not be a bad idea if the entire system works this way. If we are all careful when we deal with our own property and problems, car owners would save themselves a lot of money and headaches.

In Chinese we have a saying like this: "Sweep the snow in front of your own door, and ignore the frost on others' roofs." Though misinterpreted sometimes for selfishness, the sentence was originally advice for us to deal with our own issues instead of pointing at somebody else's similar problems. One of my favorite verses in the Bible says the same: "Why do you look at the speck of sawdust in your brother's eye and pay no attention to the plank in your own eye?" (Matthew 7:3).

If we are going to measure others with a standard, we ought to search inside first to see how we are doing against the same standard. I remember a marriage advice TV program I watched once. The host said his guests often complained: "What a pity! My wife/husband should be here to listen to this." To this the host responded: "Why focus so much on him or her being here to listen to this? If you think these words are good enough for you, go use them. If you change, your spouse will also change. If you expect only him or her to change, you both are stuck." It would be like looking for my spout stopper throughout my office when it is hidden inside the bottle.

Inspired by the Good Samaritan

by Deacon Jerry Rakosky

THE PARABLE OF THE GOOD SAMARITAN (LUKE 10:29-37) IS AN important parable of Jesus. When this parable was spoken thousands of years ago it gave the people a strong message that still applies today and will until the end of time. As we travel through our time on earth Jesus expects us to be loving and to help all people that need help even if they don't ask for our help. The Good Samaritan didn't wait for someone to tell him to go help the man who was beaten. He had a kind heart and had pity on the man even as others passed the wounded man by, even crossing to the other side of the street to avoid him.

Quite a few years ago God gave me a calling to become a Deacon in the Catholic Church. One of the ministries he guided me to was to visit the sick in nursing homes, hospitals, retirement centers, and in their homes. I spend an average of two to three days a week performing this ministry. It is a very humbling experience and at times depressing. I see the dying and those who are not capable of taking care of themselves and cannot go out. Sometimes I fill in for the Catholic chaplain at our local hospitals. Sometimes I start my day when I visit people in ICU who may be close to death and others who are extremely ill for various medical reasons, and then I finish my day by taking Communion to those on the baby floor. This allows me to sometimes observe the end of life and also the beginning of life, all in the time it takes to complete one day of hospital visits.

What I admire the most are all the Good Samaritans who work day in and day out doing what is at times I'm sure a thankless job. They work in hospitals, nursing homes, hospice centers, and as caregivers who go to people's homes. These people remind me of the Good Samaritan. Yes they do get paid, but the pay does not cover all the things they do for the people such as showing them love and concern. Most of the people are lonely like the wounded man in the Samaritan parable. In the parable the question is asked "And who is my neighbor?" These Good Samaritans can answer by saying, "It's the people I help every day." These Good Samaritans know the residents by name and help them any way they can. In my ministry as a deacon I take Communion to the Catholics and they are excited when I arrive because they know I am bringing them the "Body of Christ."

> There are many ways we all can be Good Samaritans. All we must do is look for the need. Jesus asks us to do this.

An example is one lady who suffers from Alzheimer's disease. When I go visit her every week and go into her room she doesn't recognize me or my name when I tell her it's Deacon Jerry. But when I tell her I want to give her Communion she gets excited and knows she is about to receive the "Body of Christ." She tells me over and over "Thank you, thank you. You have made my day, I need this." This is what being a Good Samaritan is all about. I enjoy leading Homebound Communion Ministers who also perform this ministry.

There are many ways we all can be Good Samaritans. All we must do is look for the need. Jesus asks us to do this. He wants us to take the path that leads to helping others and not cross the street to avoid them. Jesus gives us his mercy and love every second of every day to do this. We should give back to him for what he has given us and help his people who need us by becoming their GOOD SAMARITAN. I'm thankful for the impact this parable has had in my life.

> But because he wished to justify himself, he said to Jesus, "And who is my neighbor?" Jesus replied, "A man fell victim to robbers as he went down from Jerusalem to Jericho. They stripped and beat him and went off leaving him half dead. A priest happened to be going down that road, but when he saw him, he passed by on the opposite side. Likewise a Levite came to the place, and when he saw him, he passed by on the opposite side. But a Samaritan traveler who came upon him was moved with compassion at the sight. He approached the victim, poured oil and wine over his wounds and bandaged them. Then he lifted him up on his own animal, took him to an inn and cared for him. The next day he took out two silver coins and gave them to the innkeeper with the instruction 'Take care of him. If you spend more than what I have given you, I shall repay you on my way back.' Which of these three, in your opinion, was neighbor to the robbers' victim? He answered, 'The one who treated him with mercy.' Jesus said to him, 'Go and do likewise'" (Luke 10:29-37, NAB).

Good Examples

by Matthew Walters

But take care not to perform righteous deeds in order that people may see them; otherwise, you will have no recompense from your heavenly Father. When you give alms, do not blow a trumpet before you, as the hypocrites do in the synagogues and in the streets to win the praise of others. Amen, I say to you, they have received their reward. But when you give alms, do not let your left hand know what your right hand is doing, so that your almsgiving may be in secret. And your Father who sees in secret will repay you. When you pray, do not be like the hypocrites, who love to stand and pray in the synagogues and on street corners so that others may see them. Amen, I say to you, they have received their reward. But when you pray, go to your inner room, close the door, and pray to your Father in secret. And your Father who sees in secret will repay you. In praying, do not babble like the pagans, who think they will be heard because of their many words. Do not be like them. Your Father knows what you need before you ask him (Matthew 6:1-8, NAB).

When you fast, do not look gloomy like the hypocrites. They neglect their appearance, so that they may appear to others to be fasting. Amen, I say to you, they have received their reward. But when you fast, anoint your head and wash your face, so that you may not appear to be fasting, except to your Father who is hidden. And your Father who sees what is hidden will repay you. (Matthew 6:16-18, NAB).

THROUGHOUT TIME SOME PEOPLE HAVE CHOSEN TO PERFORM GOOD and righteous deeds for self-promotion or praise. Most of us have witnessed people practicing this. For instance, we see celebrities and politicians who use photo opportunities to fuel narcissistic tendencies or people who attend church on Sunday and fail to follow the teachings on Monday. If one believes a faux Christian lifestyle will advance their career then they will pretend to be Christians. However, I was taught the opposite: One should strive to live the Scripture while implementing its meaning throughout his life. I'm fortunate to have witnessed Matthew 6:1-8 and Matthew 6:16-18 lived out by my father and also from Father Maurice O'Connnell.

The verses from Matthew 6 helped shape me as a person as well as a Christian man. The entire chapter is read every year during Mass on Ash Wednesday at the beginning of Lent. It serves as a reminder for me and other Christians to humble ourselves and to perform righteous deeds for the grace of God. It calls upon Christians to use the basic and genuine advice of living for others and not for themselves. The Scripture gives three examples of charity, prayer, and fasting, and counsels us not to do them for the favor of others.

I first witnessed Matthew 6 modeled by my dad. I am blessed to have had wonderful Christian examples in my parents during my childhood and even now. My mother provided me with unconditional love and protection, and my father gave me the guidance all sons need. He instilled in me the values that center on the verses of Matthew 6. He follows them quietly every day. He never boasts or brags about helping those in need, he simply lets his actions do the talking for him. He attends Mass every week and volunteers at a variety of church functions. In addition he assists with activities at my niece's school. The professions he chose when he worked were ones that allowed him to spend time with and serve young people. He helped countless children during his time as a teacher, coach, principal, and alternative school director. He did the same for my sister and me as well. His example led us to choose professions that centered on helping others. I became a physical therapist and my sister is a special education teacher.

I was also blessed to know as a friend and role model the late Father Maurice O'Connell who embodied the servant leader. Father O'Connell was a priest at the Immaculate Conception Catholic

> He never boasts or brags about helping those in need, he simply lets his actions do the talking for him.

Church in Poteau, Oklahoma. I lived in Poteau during my first two years of college while attending Carl Albert State College. Father O'Connell was a lively American-Irish priest from Chicago who introduced himself to me after my first Mass there. He became a good friend and role model for me. He was active in the community during his short time in Eastern Oklahoma. He took care of the poor and he led two other parishes in neighboring towns. Other church leaders in Poteau would often call him when a need arose to care for the homeless and transients passing through. He cared for those in need often, even at the expense of one person burning down his house. He was a great mentor and helped me during my young adult life. He always felt the need to give back and to live a Christian life as a priest without the typical priestly attire. He preferred casual clothing and Birkenstock sandals and rarely wore the traditional collar. However, everyone knew Father Maurice and that they could rely on him when in need.

There are many Scriptures I look upon in my daily life that provide comfort and guidance. However the Scriptures from Matthew 6 are the most important to me. These center me and remind me what a Christian should do every day for the right reasons, and I'm glad we receive the reminder at the beginning of Lent every year.

QUICK INSPIRATION

This section is written for those hurried, on-the-go days when you desperately want to feed your soul but only have a moment to do it. These next few pages include Scriptures and brief descriptions of ways those verses helped the authors. You can read the "Quick Inspiration" pages for a fast shot of encouragement to carry you through your day.

In this section you will find verses to help you with problems we all face from time to time: worry, sin, overcoming challenges, or feeling low, inadequate, or unattractive. "God's Amazing Love" and "For Worry Over Sin" will remind you that nothing separates us from God. "Verses to Carry You Through Challenges" will emphasize the importance of living the Christian life over giving in to pressure from peers or family. And "Wonderfully Made" will lift you when you are down in the dumps. The following verses and pages hold the swift boosts of inspiration you need for your harried, crazy day, better than a dose of nine-hour-energy, for sure.

Verses to Carry You Through Challenges

by Holli Potts-Boedeker

I HAVE SO MANY FAVORITE VERSES, BUT I'LL SHARE THE ONES THAT got me through college. My friends and mentors from OCC (that is what Oklahoma Christian University was called back then) changed my life forever, and the following verses have been especially important to me since that time.

> *Even youths grow tired and weary, and young men stumble and fall; but those who hope in the Lord will renew their strength. They will soar on wings like eagles; they will run and not grow weary, they will walk and not be faint* (Isaiah 40:30-31).

These verses taught me to never give up the fight to live the Christian life—even if it means making really tough choices, ones that might go against your family, as I had to do in my late teens. This Scripture passage continues to give me strength today to overcome obstacles. It doesn't matter how old or young we are, God will help us through.

Wonderfully Made

by Melanie Hawley

My favorite Scripture passage is Psalm 139, especially verses 13 and 14:

> *For you created my inmost being; you knit me together in my mother's womb. I praise you because I am fearfully and wonderfully made; your works are wonderful, I know that full well.*

Sometimes it is easy to get down on myself or feel like I am not as good as someone else. But to think God formed me with his hands the way he wanted me to be is inspiring. God doesn't make junk; he made me in his image. I shouldn't compare myself to others but rather try to remember I am wonderfully made by HIM.

What Really Matters

by Debby McCrary

I HAD THE WORLD TUMBLING IN ON ME, AND I HAD EVERY RIGHT TO be hurt and angry. With the anger came suffering . . .and the urge to make them suffer. If I hurt, you hurt! It seemed fair, even right. Then after a time, it seemed a burden. I used all my energy making sure their suffering was evident. But I felt no satisfaction, and I was shocked that my plan wasn't giving me peace.

I believe God interrupted my plan. I needed HIM! Having God *and* my anger was like oil and water. I can't say I heard his voice, or saw a light, but one afternoon I just let go of my anger. It didn't feel like a work in progress; it felt instant. I chose forgiveness!

Now I know the feeling of having a burden lifted instantly. It was good! I was good, I felt good. Later, I was guided to a little Old Testament book and found the answer to my peace in these verses:

> HE will take great delight in you,
> HE will **quiet you with HIS love,**
> HE will rejoice over you with singing
>   (Zephaniah 3:17, emphasis added).

This is a Scripture I NEEDED my elementary school students to understand and accept. I can't say God was taking delight in me or even rejoicing with song. But . . . he did quiet me with HIS love! I am so grateful for experiencing the power of forgiveness, HIS forgiveness!

God's Amazing Love

by Myra McCrary Moran

> *Who shall separate us from the love of Christ? Shall trouble or or hardship or persecution or famine or nakedness or danger or sword? As it is written, "FOR YOUR SAKE WE FACE DEATH ALL DAY LONG; WE ARE CONSIDERED AS SHEEP TO BE SLAUGHTERED." No, in all these things we are more than conquerors through him who loved us. For I am convinced that neither death nor life, nor angels nor demons, neither the present nor the future, nor any powers, neither height, nor depth, nor anything else in all creation, will be able to separate us from the love of God, that is in Christ Jesus our Lord* (Romans 8: 35-39, emphasis added).

These have been my favorite verses ever since I was a child. They were among the first I ever memorized. It's brought me much comfort knowing that NOTHING can separate me from God's love. If you are his, the same is true for you!

Some of My Favorite Verses for Sin and Worry

by Ed Estes

Dealing with Sin

Sin is an affront to God and I have been guilty too many times. What can I do? I can try to hide from God or I can point at others and their "worse sins," which seems to make me "not so bad." Sin scars the sinner, sometimes openly and sometimes latently. Sin can also hurt and scar those around you. What can I do to reduce my sinning?

I think of the brave Prophet Nathan when he approached David and told him of his terrible sins. One of David's responses resulted in his writing of Psalm 51. Verses 10-11 are also my plea: *Create in me a clean heart, O God; and renew a right spirit within me. Cast me not away from thy presence; and take not thy holy spirit from me* (KJV).

To have a "clean heart" I want to learn what my God wants me to do. To help me to discover what that might mean, I look to Psalm 119:11: *Thy word have I hid in mine heart, that I might not sin against thee* (KJV).

For Worry Over Sin

There are times when I fret and worry about my sins. I have recurring dreams that end with me at God's judgment seat and God says to me "Ed, you have tried, but, you just can't come in." I rely on God's grace and Jesus' blood and remember Hebrews 13:5-6: *I will never leave thee, nor forsake thee. So that we may boldly say, the Lord* is *my helper, and I will not fear what man shall do unto me* (KJV).

Trust

by I. Reily

> *Trust in the Lord with all thine heart; and lean not unto thine own understanding. In all thy ways acknowledge him, and he shall direct thy paths* (Proverbs 3:5-6, KJV).

This verse is my white-knuckle verse. It's the King James Version because I studied that translation as a child. There have been a lot of things, large and small, I haven't understood, nor liked, nor expected, that made no sense to my heart . . . and to each of those God says, "Trust."

Some days I do that with gritted teeth, some days with a smile, and some days with a sigh of resignation after exhausting myself by trying everything else except trusting first.

Beauty

by Paige Bailey

> *Charm is deceptive, and beauty is fleeting; but a woman who fears the Lord is to be praised* (Proverbs 31:30).

THIS VERSE HELPED ME GET THROUGH HIGH SCHOOL AND STILL serves a big purpose in my life today. As a woman it's hard for me not to get wrapped up in people's looks and material possessions and popularity. Proverbs 31:30 helps me remember that beauty is on the inside. God is the one you should always be trying to impress and he thinks you are beautiful because of your love and fear of him.

Fear Not

by Laura McCrary

A FEW YEARS AGO, A DEAR FRIEND RECEIVED A DIAGNOSIS OF LYMPphoma cancer. The news devastated all of us in his peer group. During that time I had the blessing of working in an office with fellow Christians; I shared news of my friend's illness with them and asked for prayers on his behalf. One of my sweet co-workers led me to Isaiah 41:10:

> *So do not fear, for I am with you; do not be dismayed,*
> *for I am your God. I will strengthen you and help you;*
> *I will uphold you with my righteous right hand.*

We prayed this verse repeatedly, especially when we felt fearful or powerless about our friend's situation. As I write this, I am happy to report that he has been cancer-free for five years and his faith is stronger than ever before. God upheld my friend with his righteous hand.

I have since adopted this verse whenever I am plagued by worry or fear. The words remind me that God is always with us and he wants us to give him all our fears, weaknesses, and heavy burdens. He will strengthen and help us . . . he will uphold us with his right hand.

Notes

[1] This story is adapted from "What's Your Signature Verse?" from *Think* magazine, December 2011.

[2] Originally posted on *www.rubyforwomen.com*.

[3] Henri J. M. Nouwen, *The Return of the Prodigal Son* (New York: Doubleday, 1994), 85 (emphasis added).

[4] David E. Garland, *Colossians, Philemon – NIV Application Commentary* (Grand Rapids: Zondervan, 1998), 78.

About the Authors

PAIGE BAILEY is a wife and mother who lives with her husband and children in Oklahoma City. She and her husband are graduates of Oklahoma Christian University.

REBECCA LUTTRELL BRILEY was born and brought up in Kentucky where she received her PhD in English from the University of Kentucky. She was married to the late Kyle D. Briley and is the daughter of Christian author Wanda Moore Luttrell. Dr. Briley is the published author of several academic books and articles, as well as a collection of poetry and other creative works. Having lived and taught all over the world, she is currently writing her memoirs and marketing her novel sequel to *The Great Gatsby*.

KAY CROUCH is from Gladewater, TX. Her testimony is written to encourage all of YOU about the awesome healing power of our precious Jesus. Her love for God, Jesus, and the Holy Spirit dominate her life. She is currently leading a prayer group in her home and is active in a wonderful church home.

TIM DALLAS, PhD, is a professor of Electrical and Computer Engineering at Texas Tech University. He and his wife, Beth, have four children and reside in Lubbock, TX.

JAMES D. DVORAK is Associate Dean for Teaching and Learning and Associate Professor of Greek and New Testament at Oklahoma Christian University. He has authored numerous articles and is co-editor of *Baptism: Historical, Theological, and Pastoral Perspectives* and *The New Testament Church: The Challenge of Developing Ecclesiologies*, both published by Pickwick/Wipf and Stock.

JENNIFER ESCOBAR is a mother of three. She holds a Bachelor of Arts from Oklahoma Christian University. Wife, Mother, college graduate, and blessed beyond belief!!!!! She is "Mom" to Chloe, Allie and Emilia, and wife to Misael Escobar. She is a child of God. She loves to learn about other cultures and learn about others' life experiences. She is always a "work in progress." Through many struggles she has become "Jen" and she is finally happy with the person God has led her to be. She is excited to see where God will lead her in this life.

ED ESTES is a proud father and grandfather who lives in California with his wife.

BERLIN FANG is an instructional designer by profession, but he also writes extensively for various media outlets in China and the United States. He is now a columnist for *China Daily* and the Chinese site of *New York Times*. He translated a number of novels from English to Chinese and he has also published several collections of essays.

JACCI GANTZ has experience in middle and high school English and has taught as a full-time English instructor in Oklahoma Christian University's Lang./Lit. Dept. since the fall of 2007. She has served as a grader for Oklahoma Christian University's Education Dept. since 1996, served on OC's Bridge Program's committee, and was selected as a Timothy mentor by her OC students. She is a National Board Certified teacher, a recipient of a Fulbright Scholarship to Japan to work with elementary, junior high, high school, and universities in that country, and a Master Teacher in Language Arts for Oklahoma. Jacci has been an English consultant for the College Board Southwest region (Texas, New Mexico, Arkansas, and Oklahoma) since 1995. As an SAT scorer and presenter at statewide Language Arts conferences, she also assists English departments in developing Vertical teams within their school systems. Jacci holds a Bachelors and Masters Degree with significant progress toward her doctorate. Jacci and her husband, Logan, married in 1970 and they raised their three children in Edmond, OK. Her interests are playing with her grandchildren, Finley and Malakai, traveling with family, gardening, reading, quilting, and spending time at the lake.

MELANIE HAWLEY lives in Oklahoma. She has been blessed with a wonderful husband and two fun, energetic boys. She teaches piano lessons to fantastic students and is also able to be home with her boys. She is thankful that God has blessed her with this opportunity.

SARAH HINDS lives in Portland, Oregon, where she is a search marketing consultant. She enjoys exploring various cuisines and trying new recipes. She also spends time studying languages and traveling to new places.

ROBIN LASHLEY is from Lynchburg, Ohio. She grew up in a very small town, in the middle of a cornfield, she says. She attended Harding University in Searcy, Arkansas. After living around Orlando, Florida, for six years, she moved back to Lynchburg. She currently works at Southern State Community College as the Executive Assistant to the President and she foster parents. Parenting has been a wonderful adventure, indeed!

EMILY LINDSEY is from Portland, Oregon. She is a registered nurse who works in the ICU at the Oklahoma Heart Hospital in Oklahoma City, Oklahoma. She enjoys journaling and singing about God's grace and mercy. She is fascinated with the way God has created the human body and is intrigued by many holistic and/or alternative medical therapies. She is happily married to her best friend and incredibly thankful for the blessing of marriage.

DEBBY LAIRD McCRARY grew up in a wonderful Christian home, and had a church family along with her parents, who nurtured her and showed her God's love. Amarillo, Texas, still is a special place for her, yet God has given her abundant love of friends and family while moving with her own family. She and her husband, Marcus, have been married since 1974, and they have three children and four grandchildren. God has been faithful and HIS promises have endured.

LAURA McCRARY is a stay-at-home mother from Forney, Texas. She lives in Longview, Texas, with her husband, Jason, and son, Tyler. She is thankful to God for his grace and mercy that gets her through the day.

MYRA MORAN is in the process of being "found" in Anaheim, California, where she lives with her husband and two children. She shares bits about herself and family on Facebook and from time to time on her blog. Her free time is spent pondering what she will be when she grows up, coordinating a Mom's group at her church and dreaming up ways to redecorate and organize her apartment.

LORETTA PARRISH is a fifth generation Floridian, born in Zolfo Springs, Florida, who has also lived in Hawaii, Alabama, and Georgia before returning to Florida in 1984. She is a retired entrepreneur, having owned a professional engineering placement firm, a property development firm, and ending her career as Executive Director/owner of an adolescent drug treatment center. Writing became a passion born from having to learn to write policies, procedures, and contracts in business, as well as her intense personal study of Scriptures. Writing became the way to organize the information and "rightly divide" the truths learned. Her two daughters and three grandchildren, and the Bible classes she teaches are the other passions in her life.

HOLLI POTTS-BOEDEKER is from Katy, Texas. Her story for this book is her first writing experience on any level. She works in aviation and graduated from Oklahoma Christian University. While working in aviation, she has always been active in teaching in Bible classes at church. So, while she may not write a lot, she does translate to kids what the Bible is trying to teach. She's always trying to pass along the love for the Lord to future generations.

GWENN QUINN is the author of the book, *God, Up Close and Personal* and a regular contributing writer to *www.thechristianwoman.com*. Gwenn's writing has also appeared on other Christian websites such as *www.internetcafedevotions.com*, *www.prayerforfreedom.com*, and *www.peopleoffaith.com*. Gwenn holds a BA in Journalism and also freelance writes for secular clients. Formerly known as Gwenn McKone, Gwenn Quinn is now happily married to her wonderful husband Ed. Gwenn is mom to two terrific daughters, and besides writing, she assists her husband with his auto repair business. She can be reached at *gwenn.quinn@comcast.net*.

JERRY RAKOSKY, deacon, was born in Muskegon, Michigan. He has been married since 1962 and has five children and eight grandchildren. He has been an Ordained Deacon in the Catholic Church since 2006. His main ministry is visiting the sick in various facilities and homes. His writing experience includes preparing homilies. He retired from Oklahoma Gas and Electric Company after thirty-three years of service.

I. REILY is a free-lance illustrator who lives in Texas.

CHARLES RIX, PhD, teaches at Oklahoma Christian University. Before that he taught at New Brunswick Theological Seminary and served as the pulpit minister of the Monmouth Church of Christ in Tinton Falls, New Jersey. Prior to entering ministry Charles worked in various financial positions with ExxonMobil Corporation both domestically and overseas. He holds graduate degrees in business, theology, and philosophy, and completed his PhD in Hebrew Bible from Drew University. Charles is also a concert pianist and has given master classes and benefit recitals around the globe. As an artist, student, and teacher of Old Testament, Charles researches ways in which the Scripture speaks to the issue of human suffering. He is published in a series of essays exploring connections between the Bible, the Shoah, and the artwork of post-Holocaust painter Samuel Bak. Charles and his late wife Jenny (Alley) Rix have two children, Nathan Rix and Abby Rix Degge, both of whom hold graduate degrees and work in the disciplines of public and social policy and practice.

JOLENE SCHMIDT is from Wyandotte, Oklahoma. She loves to journal. She loves being around children, so she substitute teaches. Her hobbies include quilting, reading, traveling with her husband, and playing with her grandchildren.

GINA SIMPSON is a work-from-home mother of Isaac, Abigail, and Indiana. She and her husband, Jacob, are working to instill the Word of God in the hearts and minds of their children. She has written a few articles for *Think* magazine. She enjoys teaching children's Bible classes for the congregation that meets in Cartersville, Georgia.

MATTHEW WALTERS is a Physical Therapist from western Oklahoma. He has an Associate's degree from Carl Albert State College, a BS from Southwestern Oklahoma State University, and an MPT from the University of Oklahoma. He's been a practicing orthopedic physical therapist since 2002. Matthew has been an active member of the Catholic church all of his life. He enjoys spending time with his wife, Tina, and family. They live in Oklahoma City.

TINA WARE-WALTERS is a Spanish professor at Oklahoma Christian University. She is co-editor of and contributor to *Recipes for Success in Foreign Language Teaching: Ready-Made Activities for the L2*

Classroom. Her BA and MA are from Baylor University in Waco, Texas, and her PhD is from Texas Tech University. She and her husband, Matt, live in Oklahoma City, OK, and are in the waiting stage of the adoption process. She is the compiler and editor of *Our Favorite Verses*.

If you have a favorite Psalm and a story about how that Scripture has impacted your life, we would like to hear from you for the next collection: *Our Favorite Psalms*. You can e-mail your story, with the Scripture, to *favverses@gmail.com* with the subject heading "Our Favorite Psalms." We look forward to your submission!

Resources from Healthy Life Press

Unless otherwise noted on the site itself, shipping is free for all products purchased through *www.healthylifepress.com*.

New Releases – Fall 2014

Mommy, What's 'Died' Mean? - How the Butterfly Story Helped Little Dave Understand His Grandpa's Death, by Linda Swain Gill; Illustrated by David Lee Bass (a.k.a. "Little Dave") – Designed to assist Christian parents and other adults who love and care about children to talk with them about the difficult subject of death, the story traces a small child's experience following his grandpa's and shows how his mother sensitively answered his questions about death by using simple examples derived from the birth of a butterfly. Little Dave's story is colorfully illustrated and designed for a child and parent or trusted adult to read together. The story has been created especially for children from pre-kindergarten through 4th grade. Discussion questions are included for each story page to help determine how much the child understands. A simple imitation game is also included to help involve the child in the story. Several pages at the end of the book contain suggestions about how to discuss death and dying with children of various ages. (**Full-color printed book:** $14.99; PDF eBook: $9.99; both together: $19.99 – direct from publisher; printed books and eBooks available at *www.Amazon.com*; *www.BN.com*; *www.deepershopping.com*, and wherever books are sold.)

No Worries - Spiritual and Mental Health Counseling for Anxiety, by Elaine Leong Eng, MD – Offering a unique spiritual and mental health perspective on a major malady of our age, this practicing Christian psychiatrist has packed a dose of reality mixed with medicine and faith into a book aimed at informing, inspiring, and equipping those who wish to better help those who struggle with anxiety and related disorders, both inside and outside the church. As one endorser said, "I travel all over the world. I see fellow believers suffering from different forms of anxiety and worry. Dr. Eng's book gives me tools to recognize when people are suffering and how to encourage them to get the help they need." (Printed book: $19.99; PDF eBook: $9.99; both together: $24.99 – direct from publisher; printed books and eBooks available at *www.Amazon.com*; *www.BN. com*; *www.deepershopping.com*, and wherever books are sold.)

If God Is So Good, Why Do I Hurt So Bad?, by David B. Biebel, DMin – This **25th Anniversary Edition** of a best-selling classic (over 200,000 copies in print worldwide, in a dozen languages) is the book's first major revision since its initial release in 1989. This new version features additional original material related to the conundrum of suffering and faith (with principles learned along the way), and chapter ending questions for personal or group use. Endorser Sheila Walsh wrote, "I believe this is one of the most profound, empathetic and beautiful books ever written on the subject of suffering and loss. There is no attempt to quickly ease our pain but rather, with an understanding born in the crucible God uniquely designed for him, David offers a place to stand, a place to fall and a place to rise again. This book left an indelible mark on my heart over twenty years ago and now with this new release the gift is fresh and fragrant. I highly commend this to you!" (Printed book: $14.99; PDF eBook: $9.99; both together: $19.95 – direct from publisher; printed books and eBooks available at *www.Amazon.com*; *www.BN.com*; *www. deepershopping.com*, and wherever books are sold.)

"In this remarkable book, my friend Dave Biebel helps the reader understand exactly what's so good about God in the midst of suffering." - Joni Eareckson Tada

Earlier Releases

We've Got Mail: The New Testament Letters in Modern English – As Relevant Today as Ever! by Rev. Warren C. Biebel, Jr. – A modern English paraphrase of the New Testament Letters, sure to inspire in readers a loving appreciation for God's Word. (Printed book: $9.95; PDF eBook: $6.95; both together: $15.00 – direct from publisher; printed books and eBooks available at *www.Amazon.com*; *www.BN.com*; *www.deepershopping. com*, and wherever books are sold.)

Hearth & Home – Recipes for Life, by Karey Swan (7th Edition) – Far more than a cookbook, this classic is a life book, with recipes for life as well as for great food. Karey describes how to buy and prepare from scratch a wide variety of tantalizing dishes, while weaving into the book's fabric the wisdom of the ages plus the recipe that she and her husband used to raise their kids. A great gift for Christmas or for a new bride. (Perfect Bound book [8 x 10, glossy cover]: $17.95; PDF eBook: $12.95; both together: $24.95 – direct from publisher; printed books and eBooks available at *www.Amazon.com*; *www.BN.com*; *www.deepershopping.com*, and wherever books are sold.)

Who Me, Pray? Prayer 101: Praying Aloud, for Beginners, by Gary A. Burlingame – Who Me, Pray? is a practical guide for prayer, based on Jesus' direction in "The Lord's Prayer," with examples provided for use in typical situations where you might be asked or expected to pray in public. (Printed book: $6.95; PDF eBook: $2.99; both together: $7.95 – direct from publisher; printed books and eBooks available at *www.Amazon.com*; *www.BN. com*; *www.deepershopping.com*, and wherever books are sold.)

Resources from Healthy Life Press | 125

My Broken Heart Sings, the poetry of Gary Burlingame – In 1987, Gary and his wife Debbie lost their son Christopher John, at only six months of age, to a chronic lung disease. This life-changing experience gave them a special heart for helping others through similar loss and pain. (Printed book: $10.95; PDF eBook: $6.95; both together: $13.95 – direct from publisher; printed books and eBooks available at *www.Amazon.com*; *www. BN.com*; *www.deepershopping.com*, and wherever books are sold.)

After Normal: One Teen's Journey Following Her Brother's Death, by Diane Aggen – Based on a journal the author kept following her younger brother's death. It offers helpful insights and understanding for teens facing a similar loss or for those who might wish to understand and help teens facing a similar loss. (Printed book: $11.95; PDF eBook: $6.95; both together: $15.00 – direct from publisher; printed books and eBooks available at *www.Amazon.com*; *www.BN.com*; *www.deepershopping.com*, and wherever books are sold.)

In the Unlikely Event of a Water Landing – Lessons Learned from Landing in the Hudson River, by Andrew Jamison, MD – The author was flying standby on US Airways Flight 1549 toward Charlotte on January 15, 2009, from New York City, where he had been interviewing for a residency position. Little did he know that the next stop would be the Hudson River. Riveting and inspirational, this book would be especially helpful for people in need of hope and encouragement. (Printed book: $8.95; PDF eBook: $6.95; both together: $12.95 – direct from publisher; printed books and eBooks available at *www.Amazon.com*; *www.BN.com*; *www.deepershopping.com*, and wherever books are sold.)

Finding Martians in the Dark – Everything I Needed to Know About Teaching Took Me Only 30 Years to Learn, by Dan M. Biebel – Packed with wise advice based on hard experience, and laced with humor, this book is a perfect teacher's gift year-round. Susan J. Wegmann, PhD, says, "Biebel's sardonic wit is mellowed by a genuine love for kids and teaching. . . . A Whitman-like sensibility flows through his stories of teaching, learning, and life." (Printed book: $10.95; PDF eBook: $6.95; Together: $15.00 – direct from publisher; printed books and eBooks available at *www.Amazon.com*; *www.BN.com*; *www.deepershopping. com*, and wherever books are sold.)

Because We're Family and **Because We're Friends**, by Gary A. Burlingame – Sometimes things related to faith can be hard to discuss with your family and friends. These booklets are designed to be given as gifts, to help you open the door to discussing spiritual matters with family members and friends who are open to such a conversation. (Printed book: $5.95 each; PDF eBook: $4.95 each; both together: $9.95 [printed & eBook of the same title] – direct from publisher; printed books and eBooks available at *www.Amazon.com*; *www.BN.com*; *www.deepershopping. com*, and wherever books are sold.)

The Transforming Power of Story: How Telling Your Story Brings Hope to Others and Healing to Yourself, by Elaine Leong Eng, MD, and David B. Biebel, DMin – This book demonstrates, through multiple true life stories, how sharing one's story, especially in a group setting, can bring hope to listeners and healing to the one who shares. Individuals facing difficulties will find this book greatly encouraging. (Printed book: $14.99; PDF eBook: $9.99; both together: $19.99 – direct from publisher; printed books and eBooks available at *www.Amazon.com*; *www.BN.com*; *www.deepershopping.com*, and wherever books are sold.)

You Deserved a Better Father: Good Parenting Takes a Plan, by Robb Brandt, MD – About parenting by intention, and other lessons the author learned through the loss of his firstborn son. It is especially for parents who believe that bits and pieces of leftover time will be enough for their own children. (Printed book: $12.95 each; PDF eBook: $6.95; both together: $17.95 – direct from publisher; printed books and eBooks available at *www.Amazon.com*; *www.BN.com*; *www.deepershopping.com*, and wherever books are sold.)

Jonathan, You Left Too Soon, by David B. Biebel, DMin – One pastor's journey through the loss of his son, into the darkness of depression, and back into the light of joy again, emerging with a renewed sense of mission. (Printed book: $12.95; PDF eBook: $5.99; both together: $15.00 – direct from publisher; printed books and eBooks available at *www.Amazon.com*; *www.BN.com*; *www.deepershopping.com*, and wherever books are sold.)

Printed Cover   eBook Cover

The Spiritual Fitness Checkup for the 50-Something Woman, by Sharon V. King, PhD – Following the stages of a routine medical exam, the author describes ten spiritual fitness "checkups" midlife women can conduct to assess their spiritual health and tone up their relationship with God. Each checkup consists of the author's personal reflections, a Scripture reference for meditation, and a "Spiritual Pulse Check," with exercises readers can use for personal application. (Printed book: $8.95; PDF eBook: $6.95; both together: $12.95 – direct from publisher; printed books and eBooks available at *www.Amazon.com*; *www.BN.com*; *www.deepershopping.com*, and wherever books are sold.)

**The Other Side of Life – Over 60? God Still Has a Plan for You,** by Rev. Warren C. Biebel, Jr. – Drawing on biblical examples and his 60-plus years of pastoral experience, Rev. Biebel helps older (and younger) adults understand God's view of aging and the rich life available to everyone who seeks a deeper relationship with God as they age. Rev. Biebel explains how to: Identify God's ongoing plan for your life; Rely on faith to manage the anxieties of aging; Form positive, supportive relationships; Cultivate patience; Cope with new technologies; Develop spiritual integrity; Understand the effects of dementia; Develop a Christ-centered perspective of aging. (Printed book: $10.95; PDF eBook: $6.95; both together: $15.00 – direct from publisher; printed books and eBooks available at *www.Amazon.com*; *www.BN.com*; *www.deepershopping.com*, and wherever books are sold.)

My Faith, My Poetry, by Gary A. Burlingame – This unique book of Christian poetry is actually two in one. The first collection of poems, A Day in the Life, explores a working parent's daily journey of faith. The reader is carried from morning to bedtime, from "In the Details," to "I Forgot to Pray," back to "Home Base," and finally to "Eternal Love Divine." The second collection of poems, Come Running, is wonder,  joy, and faith wrapped up in words that encourage and inspire the mind and the heart. (Printed book: $10.95; PDF eBook: $6.95; both together: $13.95 – direct from publisher; printed books and eBooks available at *www.Amazon.com*; *www.BN.com*; *www.deepershopping.com*, and wherever books are sold.)

**On Eagles' Wings,** by Sara Eggleston – One woman's life journey from idyllic through chaotic to joy, carried all the way by the One who has promised to never leave us nor forsake us. Remarkable, poignant, moving, and inspiring, this autobiographical account will help many who are facing difficulties that seem too great to overcome or even bear at all. It is proof that Isaiah 40:31 is

as true today as when it was penned, "But they that wait upon the LORD shall renew their strength; they shall mount up with wings as eagles; they shall run, and not be weary; and they shall walk, and not faint." (Printed book: $14.95; PDF eBook: $8.95; both together: $22.95 – direct from publisher; printed books and eBooks available at *www.Amazon.com*; *www. BN.com*; *www.deepershopping.com*, and wherever books are sold.)

Richer Descriptions, by Gary A. Burlingame – A unique and handy manual, covering all nine human senses in seven chapters, for Christian speakers and writers. Exercises and a speaker's checklist equip speakers to engage their audiences in a richer experience. Writing examples and a writer's guide help writers bring more life to the characters and scenes of their stories. Bible references encourage a deeper appreciation of being created by God for a sensory existence. (Printed book: $15.95; PDF eBook: $8.95; both together: $22.95 – direct from publisher; printed books and eBooks available at *www.Amazon.com*; *www.BN.com*; *www.deepershopping.com*, and wherever books are sold.)

Treasuring Grace, by Rob Plumley and Tracy Roberts – This novel was inspired by a dream. Liz Swanson's life isn't quite what she'd imagined, but she considers herself lucky. She has a good husband, beautiful children, and fulfillment outside of her home through volunteer work. On some days she doesn't even notice the dull ache in her heart. While she's preparing for their summer kickoff at Lake George,  the ache disappears and her sudden happiness is mistaken for anticipation of their weekend. However, as the family heads north, there are clouds on the horizon that have nothing to do with the weather. Only Liz's daughter, who's found some of her mother's hidden journals, has any idea what's wrong. But by the end of the weekend, there will be no escaping the truth or its painful buried secrets. (Printed: $12.95; PDF eBook: $7.95; both together: $19.95 – direct from publisher; printed books and eBooks available at *www.Amazon.com*; *www.BN.com*; *www.deepershopping.com*, and wherever books are sold.)

From Orphan to Physician – The Winding Path, by Chun-Wai Chan, MD – From the foreword: "In this book, Dr. Chan describes how his family escaped to Hong Kong, how they survived in utter poverty, and how he went from being an orphan to graduating from Harvard Medical School and becoming a cardiologist. The writing is fluent, easy to read and understand. The sequence of events is realistic, emotionally moving, spiritually touching, heart-warming, and thought provoking. The book illustrates . . . how one must have faith in order to walk through life's winding path." (Printed book: $14.95; PDF eBook: $8.95; both together: $22.95 – direct from publisher; printed books and eBooks available at *www.Amazon.com*; *www.BN.com*; *www.deepershopping.com*, and wherever books are sold.)

12 Parables, by Wayne Faust – Timeless Christian stories about doubt, fear, change, grief, and more. Using tight, entertaining prose, professional musician and comedy performer Wayne Faust manages to deal with difficult concepts in a simple, straightforward way. These are stories you can read aloud over and over— to your spouse, your family, or in a group setting. Packed with emotion and just enough mystery to keep you wondering, while providing lots of points to ponder and discuss when you're through, these stories relate the gospel in the tradition of the greatest speaker of parables the world has ever known, who appears in them often. (Printed book: $14.95; PDF eBook: $8.95; both together: $22.95 – direct from publisher; printed books and eBooks available at *www.Amazon.com*; *www.BN.com*; *www.deepershopping.com*, and wherever books are sold.)

Unless otherwise noted on the site itself, shipping is free for all products purchased through www.healthylifepress.com.

Resources from Healthy Life Press

The Answer is Always "Jesus," by Aram Haroutunian, who gave children's sermons for 15 years at a large church in Golden, Colorado—well over 500 in all. This book contains 74 of his most unforgettable presentations—due to the children's responses. Pastors, homeschoolers, parents who often lead family devotions, or other storytellers will find these stories, along with comments about props and how to prepare and present them, an invaluable asset in reconnecting with the simplest, most profound truths of Scripture, and then to envision how best to communicate these so even a child can understand them. (Printed book: $12.95; PDF eBook: $8.95; both together: $19.95 – direct from publisher; printed books and eBooks available at *www.Amazon.com*; *www.BN.com*; *www.deepershopping.com*, and wherever books are sold.)

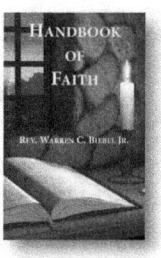

Handbook of Faith, by Rev. Warren C. Biebel, Jr. – The New York Times World 2011 Almanac claimed that there are 2 billion, 200 thousand Christians in the world, with "Christians" being defined as "followers of Christ." The original 12 followers of Christ changed the world; indeed, they changed the history of the world. So this author, a pastor with over 60 years' experience, poses and answers this logical question: "If there are so many 'Christians' on this planet, why are they so relatively ineffective in serving the One they claim to follow?" Answer: Because, unlike Him, they do not know and trust the Scriptures, implicitly. This little volume will help you do that. (Printed book: $8.95; PDF eBook: $6.95; both together: $13.95 – direct from publisher; printed books and eBooks available at *www.Amazon.com*; *www.BN.com*; *www.deepershopping.com*, and wherever books are sold.)

Pieces of My Heart, by David L. Wood – Eighty-two lessons from normal everyday life. David's hope is that these stories will spark thoughts about God's constant involvement and intervention in our lives and stir a sense of how much He cares about every detail that is important to us. The piece missing represents his son, Daniel, who died in a fire shortly before his first birthday. (Printed book: $16.95; PDF eBook: $8.95; both together: $24.95 – direct from publisher; printed books and eBooks available at *www.Amazon.com*; *www.BN.com*; *www.deepershopping.com*, and wherever books are sold.)

Dream House, by Justa Carpenter – Written by a New England builder of several hundred homes, the idea for this book came to him one day as he was driving that came to him one day as was driving from one job site to another. He pulled over and recorded it so he would remember it, and now you will remember it, too, if you believe, as he does, that ". . . He who has begun a good work in you will complete it until the day of Jesus Christ." (Printed book: $10.95; PDF eBook: $6.95; both together: $13.95 – direct from publisher; printed books and eBooks available at *www.Amazon.com*; *www.BN.com*; *www.deepershopping.com*, and wherever books are sold.)

A Simply Homemade Clean, by homesteader Lisa Barthuly – "Somewhere along the path, it seems we've lost our gumption, the desire to make things ourselves," says the author. "Gone are the days of 'do it yourself.' Really . . . why bother? There are a slew of retailers just waiting for us with anything and everything we could need; packaged up all pretty, with no thought or effort required. It is the manifestation of 'progress' . . . right?" I don't buy that!" Instead, Lisa describes how to make safe and effective cleansers for home, laundry, and body right in your own home. This saves money and avoids exposure to harmful chemicals often found in commercially produced cleansers. (**Full-color** printed book: $16.99; PDF eBook: $6.95; both together: $22.95 – direct from publisher; printed books and eBooks available at *www.Amazon.com*; *www.BN.com*; *www.deepershopping.com*, and wherever books are sold.)

The Secret of Singing Springs, by Monte Swan – One Colorado family's treasure-hunting adventure along the trail of Jesse James. The Secret of Singing Springs is written to capture for children and their parents the spirit of the hunt—the hunt for treasure as in God's Truth, which is the objective of walking the Way of Wisdom that is described in Proverbs. (Printed book: $12.95, PDF eBook: $9.99; both together: $19.99 – direct from publisher; printed books and eBooks available at *www.Amazon.com*; *www.BN.com*; *www.deepershopping.com*, and wherever books are sold.)

God Loves You Circle, by Michelle Johnson – Daily inspiration for your deeper walk with Christ. This collection of short stories of Christian living will make you laugh, make you cry, but most of all make you contemplate—the meaning and value of walking with the Master moment-by-moment, day-by-day. (**Full-color** printed book: $17.95; PDF eBook: $9.99; both together: $22.99 – direct from publisher; printed books and eBooks available at *www.Amazon.com*; *www.BN.com*; *www.deepershopping.com*, and wherever books are sold.)

Our God-Given Senses, by Gary A. Burlingame – Did you know humans have NINE senses? The Bible draws on these senses to reveal spiritual truth. We are to taste and see that the Lord is a good. We are to carry the fragrance of Christ. Our faith is produced upon hearing. Jesus asked Thomas to touch him. God created us for a sensory experience and that is what you will find in this book. (Printed book: $12.99; PDF eBook: $9.99; both together: $19.99 – direct from publisher; printed books and eBooks available at *www.Amazon.com*; *www.BN.com*; *www.deepershopping.com*, and wherever books are sold.)

Vows, a Romantic novel by F. F. Whitestone – When the police cruiser pulled up to the curb outside, Faith Framingham's heart skipped a beat, for she could see that Chuck, who should have been driving, was not in the vehicle. Chuck's partner, Sandy, stepped out slowly. Sandy's pursed lips and ashen face spoke volumes. Faith waited by the front door, her hands clasped tightly, to counter the fact that her mind was already reeling. "Love never fails." A compelling story. (Printed book: $12.99; PDF eBook: $9.99; both together, $19.99 – direct from publisher; printed books and eBooks available at *www.Amazon.com*; *www.BN.com*; *www.deepershopping.com*, and wherever books are sold.)

Worth the Cost?, by Jack Tsai, MD – The author was happily on his way to obtaining the American Dream until he decided to take seriously Jesus' command, "Come, follow me." Join him as he explores the cost of medical education and Christian discipleship. Planning to serve God in your future vocation? Take care that your desires do not get side-tracked by the false promises of this world. What you should be doing now so when you are done with your training you will still want to serve God. (Printed book: $12.99, PDF eBook: $9.99; both together: $19.99 – direct from publisher; printed books and eBooks available at *www.Amazon.com*; *www. BN.com*; *www.deepershopping.com*, and wherever books are sold.)

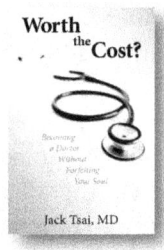

Nature: God's Second Book – An Essential Link to Restoring Your Personal Health and Wellness: Body, Mind, and Spirit, by Elvy P. Rolle – An inspirational book that looks at nature across the seasons of nature and of life. It uses the biblical Emmaus Journey as an analogy for life's journey, and offers ideas for using nature appreciation and exploration to reduce life's stresses. The author shares her personal story of how she came to grips with this concept after three trips to the emergency room. (**Full-color** printed book: $12.99; PDF eBook $8.99; both together: $16.99 – direct from publisher; printed books and eBooks available at *www.Amazon.com*; *www.BN.com*; *www.deepershopping.com*, and wherever books are sold.)

He Waited, by LaDonna Cooper – Inspires readers to wait upon the Lord for His best for them; stresses the importance of putting God's purpose above one's own; emphasizes that God's love is unconditional; demonstrates the wisdom of waiting, through a combination of positive insights, encouragement, biblical examples and principles. Decorated with original poetry by the author. For singles and others who are waiting. Distributed primarily through *www.Amazon.com*. (Printed book: $10.99; PDF eBook: $9.99; both together: $15.99 – direct from publisher; printed books and eBooks available at *www.Amazon.com*; *www.BN.com*; *www.deepershopping.com*, and wherever books are sold.)

Seasonal

The Big Black Book – What the Christmas Tree Saw, by Rev. Warren C. Biebel, Jr. – An original Christmas story, from the perspective of the Christmas tree. This little book is especially suitable for parents to read to their children at Christmas time or all year-round. (**Full-color** printed book: $9.95; PDF eBook: $4.95; both together: $12.95 – direct from publisher; printed books and eBooks available at *www.Amazon.com*; *www.BN.com*; *www.deepershopping.com*, and wherever books are sold.)

www.ingramcontent.com/pod-product-compliance
Lightning Source LLC
Chambersburg PA
CBHW052051070526
44584CB00017B/2136